...Or For Worse

Loving Your Husband Through Hard Times

By

Emma Chambers

I run in the path of your commands,

for you have set my heart free.

Psalm 119:32 NIV 1984

*To my husband, who believed
in God's healing power for
our marriage before I did.*

Contents

Acknowledgements

I am especially grateful to the members of the Suncoast Christian Writers Group for their critiques and encouragement as I worked on this book. I thank Fran Willis from that group who read through the book and offered me feedback, corrections, and insights about Bible verses. A hearty thank you also goes to Lynn Merrell, who carefully edited and proofread the book and helped me organize it. She also talked me off the "I want to quit" ledge a number of times.

My gratitude goes to those who broadcast three radio show programs, which helped me when I felt discouraged in married life. They believed and helped me to believe in the permanence of marriage and in God's ability and desire to heal troubled marriages. They are *Revive Our Hearts* with Nancy DeMoss Wolgemuth, *Family Life Today* with Dennis Rainey and *Focus on the Family* with James Dobson and these days Jim Daly.

I want to thank the former Florida Christian Writers Conference director, Billie Wilson, and the staff and numerous editors and authors who came there and encouraged me all along on my path as a writer and a Christian. Two editors from there are Andy Scheer and Cynthia Schnereger, who helped me have the courage to write about difficult areas of my marriage in articles, which they published in *Moody* and *Light and Life* magazines. Two authors I met at writers conferences who have been a continued source of encouragement to me as a writer and as a wife are Sandy Sheppard and Fran Sandin.

Thanks also goes to the fellow board members of Growth in Faith who truly helped me grow in faith, prayed many prayers for me when I felt desperate, and offered words of encouragement and shoulders to cry on during my hard times in marriage and in life in general.

Thank You, Marie Yates, for teaching me how to recognize God's voice and reminding me again and again to "ask the Father." Thank you to all the members of Marie's Tuesday morning Bible study who prayed, encouraged me with truth, and let me know they knew how I felt—that I was not alone. Thank you also for all your prayers for this book project.

I also want to thank my parents who have been married for sixty-seven years and despite many hardships have showed me what unconditional love looks like in marriage.

Thank you to my husband who also believes in the permanence of marriage and has forgiven me again and again and lifted me up when I've been the one to lose my way. I thank him for the courage to allow me to write and speak about our marriage to help others in theirs.

Most importantly, I thank the Lord, who repeatedly cheers and encourages me and brings miracle after miracle into my marriage and into my life. Thank You for the privilege of knowing, loving, and serving You.

Introduction

When I finally mustered up courage to tell other Christian wives I no longer dwelled in the better, but had entered the worse times in my marriage, I mostly received one of two responses: "That's too bad," or "You should get a divorce." Some feebly said, "I'll pray for you." Rarely did I hear, "God can heal your marriage."

The truth I discovered from other sources changed the course of my life. God *can* heal any marriage and through this book, I want to proclaim that truth and celebrate God as healer.

God healed our marriage and continues to do so; we now look forward to celebrating 43 years together. The Lord showed me a richer life beyond the only options which seemed available: the role of desperate housewife or divorcee.

I learned all things are possible with God—including healing a marriage going through hard times with problems which appeared insurmountable. God drew me closer to Him, so I could hear Him whisper, "If you determine to remain the loving one, the obedient one, I will heal your marriage, even if your husband doesn't seem willing to cooperate."

God made Romans 12:2 real in my life: "Do not conform to the pattern of this world, but be transformed by the renewing of your mind..." He helped me relinquish the miracle I desperately wanted—a changed husband. Instead He opened my heart to the miracle of change in me—a transformed mind which resulted in the ability to think differently about marriage than our culture or worldly Christians, and the capacity to think and act like Him. Then my love for my husband flourished—even in difficult times. Rather than demand my husband change and love me in my prescribed way, I learned the art of unconditional love.

Today I celebrate the change in my perspective and my arrival at this truth: my marriage is not all about me, but about God and giving Him glory by becoming more like Him--especially in hard times.

Repeatedly God reminds me the enemy of my marriage isn't my husband, but Satan. By His power, God helped me obliterate every lie the ugly one tried to tell me about our marriage, especially "Your marriage cannot be saved."

Whenever I felt certain I would drown in the rough waters of marriage, God reminded me of His presence. During those times I discovered the great joy found in praising God in the hard times. To praise Him instead of complaining about circumstances helped me endure hard times. Often I think of Isaiah 43:2 as it applies to difficult times in marriage: "When you pass through the waters, I will be with you; and when you pass through the rivers, they will not sweep over you. When you walk through the fire, you will not be burned; the flames will not set you ablaze."

My "way through" rather than "way out" thinking in marriage transformed me into a better person and a stronger Christian. God taught me what joy awaits me when I embrace way-through thinking. To face a problem and believe it's possible, with God's help, to get to the other side, no matter how long it takes or how much it hurts, built my character. To admit my mistakes, repent, and suffer the consequences while I received God's mercy increased my perseverance. When I live like this, I feel myself growing up, and it's a satisfying feeling. I discovered the key to a God-glorifying marriage lies not in being loved but in learning to love like Jesus.

Before my transformation, hopelessness ruled my life. God transported me from hopelessness to this declaration: "He is my hope." God didn't promise me a changed husband, but a transformed life if I embraced His truths. I found a different level of happiness, one not based on circumstances but on an increased dependence on the Lord, as spelled out in the truth of this verse: "He who pays attention to the word [of God] will find good, And blessed (happy, prosperous, to be admired) is he who trusts [confidently] in the LORD" (Proverbs 16:20 AMP).

I discovered my ungodly reactions to my husband's negative behaviors contributed to my marital misery. Our pastor stated this truth in a sermon: "The most miserable person in the world is not the person who is not saved. The most miserable person is the Christian who is not in God's will."

God's will always involves loving and doing the next loving action. Too often in marriage when I hurt, I moved away from that pursuit. Thankfully, I learned the joy of a godly response— even when I hurt. One avenue to a godly response came when I learned to ask God questions like: "How do I love my husband today?" and "What do I do now?" I heard His response and followed it.

One danger I faced in my darkest days of marital trouble lay in my refusal to pray, seek God in His Word, or interact with fellow Christians. This isolation from God and His people increased my sense of failure in our marriage.

I learned the importance of staying connected to the Lord and to carefully-chosen fellow Christians. The encouragement I received there I passed along to other hurting wives, many who faced more desperate situations than mine.

My husband and I still struggle with issues. Not long ago we went for months of marriage counseling, which helped immensely. Suffering from abusive backgrounds, both of us continue to battle effects of the traumas we experienced. But God repeatedly shows His faithfulness. This book is the story of God's faithfulness in our marriage.

Years ago I read this quote which has stayed with me, "God is no respecter of persons, but He is a respecter of faith." Along the way, God helped me increase my faith in Him, which opened the door to receive all He had for me—including a healed marriage. He wants to do the same for you.

I want to be the living, loving example of Jesus through how I love my husband. Writing this book helped me in that endeavor, especially as the Lord led me to the "love verses" in 1 Corinthians 13 and showed me how to truly apply them to my marriage.

My heart longs to fully embrace the quest of loving my husband for a life time—even in hard times. It's sometimes difficult, but well worth it. And if I stay on the path the Lord shows me, He supplies plenty of joy for the journey. I pray what I learned along the way will help you to love your husband—even in hard times. –Emma Chambers

A Word About Physical Abuse

While this book isn't written specifically for wives in violent marriages, the truths presented here can work to end abuse. The goal is to stay married and never get hit again. However, allowing yourself to receive abuse is not a part of God's picture of submission. If you're physically abused, it's essential to get to a place of safety.

A book I recommend is *Angry Men and the Women Who Love Them—Breaking the Cycle of Physical and Emotional Abuse* (Beacon Hill Press © 1999) by Paul Hegstrom, Ph.d. Paul verbally and physically abused his wife for fifteen years before he received God's truth and was set free. In his book he emphasizes: "One thing we must not fail to understand is that if someone is abusing us, we have the right to remove ourselves from that situation." (From Kindle DX, 25%/547/Chapter Three)

Part I

Can This Marriage Be Saved?

…with God all things are possible.
—Matthew 19:26b NIV

I want my life and my marriage to look less like the
world and more like Christ. —Marquis Clarke

Chapter 1

Lisa and Chris's Story

The rain beat against the windshield as Lisa stared out onto the road ahead. She wondered why she agreed to come along when Chris said, "Let's move to Florida."

How could you? she thought for the 1000th time in recent days. Hiding her panic beneath anger, she turned to glare at her husband as he drove.

His unfaithfulness—his adultery, crushed her.

"It was only once," he insisted.

All her dreams for marriage lay crumbled. Chris was to be the person who would love her perfectly—the way she wanted her parents to love her. Now his "I love yous" seemed hollow.

"What are you thinking about?" Chris asked.

He reached for her hand. Lisa turned away and ignored him for many miles, and recalled the hurtful words he hurled at her after he confessed to his affair weeks before.

"I don't think I ever really loved you, Lisa." "It was a mistake for us to get married." "She wants me to leave you and marry her."

Lisa replayed the day Chris confessed. She tearfully packed belongings into her car and drove to a friend's house, thinking she'd never return. She felt humiliated to discover the friend

3

knew about Chris reconnecting with a former girlfriend at a party while Lisa worked the evening shift.

She remembered the moment Chris called her at the friend's house and begged her to come home. The "other woman" decided to stay with her husband and make things work. Lisa still felt deep love for Chris, so despite her anger and hurt, she returned home.

Now, Lisa contemplated the state of her two-year-old marriage while watching raindrops make their way down the windshield. She wondered, *Why did I go back? To be his second choice? Someone to cook his dinner and wash his clothes?* Even though he said, "I was wrong; I do love you," Lisa found it difficult to believe that or anything he said.

I shouldn't be here," Lisa finally spoke. "There's no hope for us."

Chris was silent a moment, then asked, "What about Jesus? You talk about Him a lot. Can't Jesus save this marriage?"

Chapter 2

Saying "Yes" To Jesus

On that rainy day two years into her marriage somewhere on Interstate 75 on her way from Illinois to Florida, minutes after Chris asked, "What about Jesus?" Lisa opened her heart to Him. She gave Him the mess she made trying to fix her life and her marriage. She gave Him all her sins and faults, and asked that He be her Savior.

Although she talked about Him and went to church and read the Bible, Jesus didn't move into her heart until that day when she invited Him to do so with a prayer that went something like this: "I'm sorry for what I've done wrong in my life and I ask for forgiveness. Thank You for dying on the cross for me to set me free from my sins. Please come into my life and fill me with your Holy Spirit and be with me forever. Amen."

Lisa said "yes" to Jesus and at the same time "yes" to Chris's second question. It was not yet something she felt; rather it was something she knew. "Yes, He can save this marriage."

She reached for Chris's hand.

The healing in Lisa's marriage took time and work. Some problems remain. Lisa's healing in her personal life and in her marriage goes on.

Admitting her part in the problem was key to healing her marriage. She took on extra evening hours after working a full day to prevent spending any more time with her husband than absolutely necessary. Even before her husband's affair, she longed for more attention, deeper intimacy, and greater tenderness from her husband. She tried to demand them, and when that didn't work, she took a second job to avoid facing and working through the disappointments of married life.

Lisa now loves her husband with a deeper love than she ever dreamed possible—even more than on their wedding day. And she's grown closer to the Lord than she ever imagined. She now reaps the benefits of holding tightly to God and His Word while praying diligently through troubled times. She discovered that going through hard times in marriage while clinging to the Lord made her into a better person. Sacrificial love does that.

Lisa learned God needed her to participate in the healing of their marriage and allow Him to help her love her husband through every difficulty they faced.

Soon Lisa and Chris will celebrate 43 years of marriage.

In case you haven't guessed it, the couple in the Chris and Lisa story are my husband and me. Since that day, God has done miracles in our lives—because I said that first "yes" way back then and continue to say "yes" to the Lord when it comes to marriage and how He wants me to love my husband.

Chapter 3

A Change in Attitude

Even after my "yes," I discovered marriage is hard, but God is good and longed to help me love my husband—no matter what he did.

Happiness Was My Number One Goal

Nancy DeMoss Wolgemuth writes about the kind of wife I was for too many years of our marriage in her book, *Lies Women Believe* (Moody Press 2001):

"Her life revolves around herself—her happiness and her hurts. She is more interested in getting her problems solved and her needs met than in the process of restoration and sanctification—in how God could use her as an instrument of grace in her husband's life...She has left God out of the picture. She does not see His holy purposes for her marriage. Nor does she see how her husband's flaws and the difficulties in her marriage could contribute toward those purposes. She is not exercising faith in the supernatural power of God to transform her and her husband and this marriage into something of great beauty and worth" (page 158).

I thought the key to my happiness lay in getting my husband to love me the way I wanted him to love me. His lack of response to my attempts to teach him how to love me and make me happy frustrated and at times infuriated me.

Along the way God showed me higher goals than "to be loved," and "to be happy:" "to love" and "to make others happy." With God's help, I can accomplish those goals.

Learning From Jesus

As I learned from Jesus, I changed. I discovered an attitude change in a wife can save a marriage. One way to a new attitude toward my husband and marriage is to move from "my marriage" and start calling it "our marriage." It also helps to see it as "God's marriage."

As I sought God with all my heart, I admitted, "I don't know how to love my husband; please teach me." God brought me to the place where I could declare, "God loves my husband just as much as He loves me—no matter what my husband does." Another admission was, "I'm part of the problem."

Three New Objectives

God presented to me three keys to help my marriage:

1. Close the divorce door.
2. Make new goals.
3. Draw near to God.

#1 Close the Divorce Door

I removed the divorce door completely from our marriage and determined to avoid the mention of the word. Even if times seemed horrible, I refused to prop the divorce door open and cherish the option of, "If things get really bad, I'll just get a divorce." I realized this mindset could keep me from investing fully in our marriage and giving myself wholeheartedly to my husband.

#2 Make New Goals

I let go of "Be happy," or "Get my husband to love me perfectly." Instead I embraced two new goals. Goal # 1 was "Love my husband." Part of loving my husband centered on letting go of the fantasy man I compared him to in my mind. Most Christian women agree they don't want their men fantasizing about naked women. Yet we tend to fantasize about "naked" men—not ones who bare their bodies, but who bare their souls to us—something many husbands shrink from doing.

Goal #2 is: "Make God Happy." I discovered when I obeyed God by loving my husband even when it seemed I wasn't loved in return, I blessed God. I realized this made Him happy because that's the kind of love He demonstrates toward each of us.

#3 Draw Near To God

At first I found it hard to "go to God" because I felt angry at Him; I blamed Him for my husband's faults and wondered why my prayers remained unanswered to keep this sorry specimen of a man from making me unhappy. As I drew close to God, He taught me how to love my husband and how to change my attitude toward him. And I loved the closeness I felt toward God as I fully embraced James 4:8: "Come near to God and he will come near to you…"

I discovered true love centers on facing the rugged journey of matrimony together. And even if my husband chooses to be unwilling to face the journey wholeheartedly with me, the Lord certainly will.

God, help me to believe in Your power to heal our marriage. Empower me to cooperate fully as You show me how to love my husband—even in hard times. In Jesus' name I pray. Amen.

Part II

Embracing "As Long As We Both Shall Live."

Love never fails [it never fades nor ends].
—1 Corinthians 13:8 AMP

Marriage is the life long journey of learning
to love like Christ." —unknown

Chapter 4

Letting Go Of Other Vows

When Christian women told me of their decision to divorce, a question often came to mind. In my times of despair when I wanted to give up, the Lord whispered this same question to me:

What about your marriage vows?

I made promises on my wedding day—before God and a crowd of people we loved—promises to love unconditionally and forever. How sincere I felt when I recited these words:

"I take you, Randy, to be my husband to have and to hold from this day forward, for better or for worse, for richer, for poorer, in sickness and in health, to love and to cherish; from this day forward until death do us part."

Yet those words seemed to mean little when I faced "or for worse" times of our marriage, often because I became entangled in the world's view of love and marriage, which is "as long as we both shall love" or "as long as we both feel happy."

Vows Outside the Marriage Vows

I discovered one reason I found it hard to keep my wedding day vows was because I made vows outside of those—promises which often won out over promises of forever love. These promises I made to myself centered on withholding love under certain conditions. Usually these other vows started out with, "If my husband ever…" and ended with "I will not put up with it," or "I'll leave him." These subconscious vows, what some call "inner vows," seldom surface until a time of deep soul-searching.

Randy and I came into our marriage with these other vows, ones just as dangerous as other women or another man. I made these vows to protect myself—contracts with my flesh to avoid hurt. Such vows are Satan's counterfeit of godly vows (which are promises to God) written of in the Bible: "Sacrifice thank offerings to God, fulfill your vows to the Most High" (Psalm 50:14).

Marriage Without Other Vows

Because I carried unrealistic expectations into marriage, I mistakenly thought inner vows would help me attain my lofty goals. My mother celebrates a successful 67-year marriage because she didn't have such unrealistically high expectations which she says belong to my generation. She lived in an orphanage from ages five to twelve. Because of this, she didn't take a roof over her head, clothes on her back and plenty of food to eat for granted. Because her husband, my father, provided food, clothing, and shelter, she knew he loved her. She views anything above that as a bonus.

Letting Go of the Fairy Tale Marriage Vow

One trap I fall into centers on this thought: *I'm supposed to feel happy all the time.* This thought comes because I made a vow of "I'm going to have a happily ever after marriage."

In her article, "My Fairy Tale Marriage," (*Today's Christian Woman*, June 2012) Tammy Bovee expresses that "we can love better when we let go of our romantic dreams." She began her marriage with such dreams. She writes: "I believed, like so many romantic stories advocate, my prince charming would fulfill all my fairytale dreams. As we climbed into our own car and Jeff drove us into the sunset, I imagined we were entering our 'happily ever after.'" But as their marriage progressed, Tammy and her husband faced severe financial issues, among others, which threatened their marriage. After giving up her fairy tale dreams, she found mature love.

"Instead of expecting my husband to meet all my needs, somewhere along the way, I learned to make God my source. Surrendering my dreams to God freed me to love Jeff for all the wonderful things he is. Today we share a wealth of comfort and companionship that comes only through persevering together. I have to admit; this reality exceeds even fairytale fantasies."

Other Vows Randy and I Made

In counseling, I discovered my number one vow which affected our marriage: "No one's going to hurt me the way my father did."

I asked Randy about his.

"No one's going to control me the way my mother did," he answered without hesitation.

As we looked carefully at how these vows worked in our marriage, we saw he carried out his "I won't let her control me"

15

vow through anger and withdrawal from me—which I found hurtful. Consequently I tried to deal with his anger and/or withdrawals through even further attempts to control him—which made him angrier and caused him to withdraw even more. Thus the vicious cycle went for years. It escalated until we uncovered and renounced the inner vows we made. But still, if we're not alert, we slip back into this cycle.

It's good to check periodically for any vows or promises which may lurk in the deep recesses of my mind, such as:

- I refuse to stay with a man who lies to me.
- I can be married only to a man who prays with me.
- I'm gone if he speaks hatefully to me.

These vows remained hidden during hard times, and led to thoughts deep inside that said, *I don't love him anymore* and even at times, *I have to leave my husband.*

The Vow to Change Him

A major area for such vows came when I wanted to change my husband. I found issues I didn't like before we married, so I made prenuptial promises like "Once we're married, I'll get him to change that." Areas for this kind of vow included drinking, smoking, TV-watching habits, temperament, messiness, and others.

When my husband didn't cooperate with my vows, my heart-hardening began. And a hard heart eventually proclaims, "I don't love him anymore." The tricky aspect of vows came when they hurt my prayer life because I made them without God in the equation. Once I renounced the vows I made, my prayer life flourished, and God began to work mightily.

Chapter 5

The Purpose of Marriage

As I let go of my view of marriage which centered on my need to feel loved and happy every moment, God showed me His view of marriage as a reflection of His love. Every time I loved my husband when it seemed he didn't deserve it, God whispered, "That's how I love you." When others knew of my struggles, I spoke about God's unconditional love and how He used my marriage to train me to love like Him.

He also revealed marriage as a covenant and not just a contract. Here is what Dennis Rainey says about the subject:

"Marriage has become little more than an upgraded social contract between two people—not a holy covenant between a man and a woman and their God for a lifetime. In the Old Testament days, a covenant was the most sacred and solemn of pledges. When two people entered into a covenant with one another, a goat or lamb would be slain and its carcass would be cut in half. With the two halves separated and lying on the ground, the two people who had formed the covenant would solemnize their promise by walking between the two halves saying, 'May God do so to me [cut me in half] if I ever break this covenant with you and God!'" (Dennis Rainey from Crosswalk.com, October 8, 2002)

Since God loves me with an everlasting love, that's how He wants me to love my husband. He showed me that marriage isn't about self-fulfillment but fulfillment of God's will.

Most of the answers I discovered about love and marriage I found in the Word of God, which teems with ways to apply God's will to marriage and to loving my husband. Unfortunately when hard times come, I often find it difficult to turn to the Word. The enemy works hard to keep me from God's Word and instead urges me to concentrate on the negative words which race through my mind.

I try to always keep in mind that the true battle is not against my husband, but against the enemy of my soul and of my marriage. The Word tells me his goals in John 10:10: "The thief comes only to steal and kill and destroy." Jesus has different goals. He says, "I have come that they may have life, and have it to the full" (verse 10b) The Lord presents me with his question repeatedly: "With whom will you cooperate—Me or the enemy?"

What Will Be The Reason?

As I observed Christian marriages around me, I saw couples give up quickly and easily, jumping into divorce before they considered other options. I boldly asked Christians wives who chose that option, "Why did you get a divorce?" I wondered, *If I got a divorce, what would my reason/excuse be?*

Two common answers came: "I didn't have the strength to go on," or "It was an impossible situation."

For the first answer, a Scripture popped into my mind, "I can do all this through him who gives me strength" (Philippians 4:13). For the second, God's Word came quickly to me, "…with God all things are possible" (Matthew 19:26)

(For a more complete list of reasons women give for divorce with a correlating scripture, see Appendix 1 titled "Reasons To Stay Married.")

Withdrawing Your Love

Often I insisted I would never get divorced, but instead I withdrew love from my husband, coexisting in our home without the deep love connection we once enjoyed.

I promised myself, "I'll love him again if and when he changes." I saw the danger of that attitude when I thought how easy it would be for my husband to meet a woman who communicated, "I love you just the way you are."

I felt justified in my reasons for withholding love from my husband. Rather than giving in to withdrawal, God taught me to do battle with such proclamations of unbelief through His Word. Instead of insisting my husband change, I allowed God to change me. Here's a little poem I wrote on the subject:

> Lord, change him has been my plea.
> "He has such faults, Lord; can't You see?"
> But the course of my heart should rather be
> learning to pray, "Lord, change me."

God used hard times to accomplish the transformation process in my heart. In her book *How To Act Right When Your Spouse Acts Wrong*, (Waterbrook Press 2001) Leslie Vernick writes: "...God uses the imperfections, differences, and sins of your spouse to help you grow to be more like Christ...Learning to respond rightly when we are wronged and wounded takes maturity and wisdom—and hard work. God is interested in developing the character of Christ within us." (Kindle DX 3% & 4%/109 & 122/Introduction)

Take A Look at Your Parents.

Many Christian women I meet see divorce as the only solution because their mothers did. Fortunately, my parents have stayed married for 60some years, despite many difficulties. Randy's parents were married for 49 years when his father died of cancer. We saw love prevail through troubled times in our parents' marriages as they dealt with mental illness, problems with rage, controlling spouses, and other issues.

Our parents' perseverance helps us hold on no matter what difficulties come. Yet I discovered even if other wives come from a long line of divorced or loveless marriages, they can determine to be the first of a long line of healthy, God-glorifying marriages.

Entering Marriage With Wounds.

Randy and I entered our marriage wounded. Randy's view of women can be connected to "Spanky and Our Gang"—old short films we watched on television as children. The boys in the "gang" had a club called "The He-Man Womun Haters Club." If a similar club for girls existed, I would have been a member and possibly president.

In our childhood, neither of us received adequate love or had our needs met from the opposite sex parent. We also suffered serious rejections in our dating years.

Over time I learned to take time to examine my baggage and make efforts to part with it. Instead of the goals of "dump my husband" or "move to the other side of house," I considered carefully the issues and "other vows" that kept us fighting, putting each other down, or participating in other destructive behaviors.

20

Despite our backgrounds and our inner vows connected to them, God intervened in marvelous ways over the years to bring us to the place of forever love.

Lord, reveal to me any vows I made, and help me let go of them and fully embrace my wedding vows. Help me believe Your love can flow through me to my husband, so I can love Him forever—the way You love me. In Jesus' name I pray. Amen.

Part III

Winning "I Don't Love Him Anymore" Attacks

Love is patient, love is kind. It does not envy, it does not boast, it is not proud. It does not dishonor others, it is not self-seeking, it is not easily angered, it keeps no record of wrongs. Love does not delight in evil but rejoices with the truth. It always protects, always trusts, always hopes, always perseveres. Love never fails...
—1 Corinthians 13:4-8

Whoso loves believes the impossible.
—Elizabeth Barrett Browning

Chapter 6

When Feelings Fade

I just don't love my husband anymore.

How often I thought and felt that.

One author suggested burnout can lead to this "no longer in love" feeling. It also happens in other areas of our lives, such as motherhood. I chose not to put my children up for adoption when I found it difficult to love them. When I feel burned out on my job, I refrain from stomping away from the career I once loved. God taught me to deal with issues at the core of burnout. I take breaks. I determine to find ways to cope with stressors in the workplace or with my children.

Those "I no longer love this man" feelings strike me more often than I like, preceded by "I don't think he loves me anymore." "No love" feelings come when Randy fails to meet my needs or when he hurts me deeply, and the pain of rejection lingers too long.

Somewhere along the way, God taught me how much *He* loves me. He urged me to receive that love and pass it along to my husband—even in his most unloving moments. Since God's love is everlasting, if I love my husband with God's love, then my love for my husband will never die. With God's love alive in me, my marriage vows of "For better *or for worse*" remain intact.

The Love-Tester

An acquaintance introduced me to an issue which hindered the flow of love from me to my husband.

"Your problem is you're a love-tester," this wiser, older man told me years ago. "This is how it works," he explained. "Finish this sentence: 'If you loved me, you would...'"

I related it to marriage so I said, "If my husband loved me, he would..."

"Now list all the things you wish your spouse would do, but doesn't," he said. "Because he's failing in each of these, he has flunked the love test you set up in your mind."

It amazed me how often I became trapped in this behavior.

Once, in a marriage class at a women's retreat, the speaker advised that married couples should do certain things together. I made a list.

If Randy loved me he would make sure we go to church together, pray together, eat meals together, go out alone together, sleep in the same bed together. At the time we had extra stressors: opposite schedules, and providing care for our granddaughter. But still, he was failing at together time.

Self-pity moved in, and my first thought was to withdraw from Randy even more. Instead, when I realized my relapse into love-testing, I wrote down what we did together. I also confessed I avoided certain together activities—like doing yard work or going to the store or some other outing, because I didn't feel like it or desired more meaningful times together. As far as sleeping together, we tried, and because of snoring, me being a light sleeper, and his erratic sleep schedule, sleeping apart proved to be for the best.

Once I moved away from love-testing in this area of togetherness, God helped me to think about, pray about, and communicate with Randy regarding solutions instead of getting lured back into thoughts of, "He doesn't love me," and then "I don't think I love him either." Now that Randy is retired, our "what we do together" list has expanded.

I ask God to keep me alert for the return of these love-testing ways.

Chapter 7

Lord, Show Me How To Love This Man

In hard times, rather than proclaim, "I just don't love this man anymore," I learned to pray "Lord, how do I love this man?" God, who is love, faithfully answers every time.

An older woman I befriended in a Bible study showed her husband—an alcoholic who determined to continue drinking—a love I'll never forget. Whenever Arlene asked for prayer for her husband, she always said his name in such a loving way.

"How do you keep on loving Howard even though he won't allow God to set him free from alcohol? I asked her one day.

"Whenever I feel I don't have a bit of love left in me, I pray to God and ask Him to give me new zeal for loving him. He's always faithful to do just that," she answered quickly.

I prayed Arlene's prayer, and it worked! Recently I looked up the word "zeal" in my dictionary: "Eagerness and ardent interest in pursuit of something: fervor, passion," I read.

One way God gives me new zeal to love my husband happens when I ask Him to speak to me about my husband or "give me a picture of him."

One day when Randy lashed out at me with harsh words, I pictured him as a monster trying to claw at my soul. I asked

God, "How do you see my husband?" The answer He gave changed my perspective:

"I see him as a hurt child."

My Husband/ My Friend

Randy often says, "You're my best friend," even though I've wanted him to say, "you are the love of my life."

God showed me the correct approach to loving my husband was as a friend. My husband's appreciation deepened when I presented myself as his friend. Perhaps the foundation of a man's perception that his wife loves him is her friendship. Randy said it was true for him. I also thought of women who mourned over not enough romance in the marriage. What I realized is Randy needs friendly love just as much as I need romance. How often I demanded romance from him, but I didn't act like his friend—laughing with him, showing interest in what he likes, and valuing his opinions.

Loving Differently

Men love differently or at the very least, my husband loves differently than I do. If I were to ask Randy, "What were the loving things you did for me today?" he would say, "I went to work and provided for you. I bought you what you like at the store. I replaced the burned-out light bulb for you." But since I think of romance and sweet words as ways to show love, my list differs.

I need to consider what makes my husband feel loved rather than what I consider as love. Years ago I went to the Lord and asked Him to give me three solid ways to show love to Randy that would work throughout our marriage. The answers God gave me were:

1) Listen—really listen—to him,
2) Don't try to change him, and
3) Greet him enthusiastically when he walks through the door.

As I consider these three instructions, I see these are ways I treat my women friends.

However, I struggle with all three with Randy. But when I told him of this list, he agreed wholeheartedly with them—that he felt loved when I did these things.

Embracing God's Love List

Kim Sadler, a counselor in the Daytona Beach area states "Couples want to know, 'What can I do to stop hurting?' Sometimes it's 'I'm hurting, and it's my spouse's fault. How can we fix him, so I can stop hurting?' We want a list. God has given us the list—in the love verses. He is saying, 'Be like Me.' The problem is we don't want to do the list."

As I cried out to God to instill love in me for my husband, He brought me to 1 Corinthians 13. Out of the truths of these verses spring loving actions which keep love alive. I used to like to read these words aloud, hear them at weddings, hang them on my wall in the form of a plaque, but living them remained a challenge I often refused to fully embrace.

Although I knew these verses and the virtues contained in them in the beginning of our marriage, God showed me my lack of them in my heart. Along the way the Lord taught me how to open my heart, receive, and live out these qualities in my life. They are: patience, compassion, contentment, humility, respect, submission, gentleness, forgiveness, encouragement, faith, endurance, and hopefulness. Jesus demonstrates these qualities in abundance. I've discovered them in hard times as I offered to God a humble, teachable heart.

When I embraced these attributes and began to love my husband in a new way—the way Christ loves me—God guaranteed me blessings on this journey as I let go of, "I don't love him anymore." Instead of moving away from my husband in my heart, I moved toward loving him with Christ's love flowing through me. As a bonus, Christ's love first flowed to me, and touched my heart, bringing me great joy and peace.

God, whenever I get the feeling, "I don't love him anymore," remind me that it's just a feeling. Help me to stop being a love-tester, and let me believe Your love as described in 1 Corinthians 13 can flow through me to my husband. In Jesus' name I pray. Amen.

Part IV

Willing To Wait

Love is patient… —1 Corinthians 1:4

Patience must be the charm to heal me of my woe.
—Sir Thomas Wyatt

Chapter 8

Weary of Waiting

I don't think it's arbitrary or coincidental that God started out the love verses in 1 Corinthians 13 with "Love is patient." The longer I'm on planet earth, the more I see love and waiting are tied together.

I'm so weary of waiting is a phrase which runs through my mind often. One area is praying my husband will develop a passion for God. Although he received Jesus as his savior and attends church, he often resists God and easily strays into ungodliness and worldliness. One of the obstacles he has in drawing near to God is that when his mother did that, she became mentally ill—going into a psychiatric hospital convinced she was the Virgin Mary. Satan set up fears in his mind, which seemed impossible to overcome.

I so relate to David in the Psalms when he prayed: "How long, Lord?" (See Psalm 6:3, 13:1, 35:17, 89:46) My *how long, Lord?* groans seem to go unheeded. Then when it appears my husband has changed and is seeking the Lord, Satan will drag him back into the pit. Randy can seem like a prodigal, and I long for him to come home. Instead of waiting, praying and believing, too often my course has been to try to drag my prodi-

35

gal home. That doesn't work. Instead it can set up even more resistance.

One verse I hold to is, "he who began a good work in you will carry it on to completion until the day of Christ Jesus" (Philippians 1:6).

Patience in Marriage

I've realized I can spend time waiting, but not do it patiently. When I looked up "patient" in my dictionary I read: "bearing pains or trials calmly or without complaint; manifesting forbearance under provocation or strain; steadfast despite opposition, difficulty or adversity."

I saw those statements as goals. Although I've come a long way, I still haven't fully arrived at being a patient wife. The good news is the Lord wants to help me be a patient wife and will guide me on that course: "May the Lord direct your hearts into the love of God and into the steadfastness and patience of Christ…" (2 Thessalonians 3:5 AMP).

Our Theme Verse

What's helped me grow in patience is a promise God gave me for our marriage, what I sometimes call our theme verse: "He has made everything beautiful in its time" (Ecclesiastes 3:11). Whenever I start to get impatient again, the Lord reminds me of that verse, and I think, *Certain areas of our marriage aren't beautiful, because it's not time yet; God's not finished with us there.*

As I become willing to wait, good things happen—especially in my heart. The Word explains it this way: "But they that wait upon the LORD shall renew their strength; they shall mount up with wings as eagles; they shall run, and not be weary; and they shall walk, and not faint" (KJV).

As I pray and wait for my husband to become more Christlike—to become all God has called him to be—I hold to what my Bible study teacher says repeatedly, "Faith is waiting in thanksgiving."

Truths to Accept

I've seen the importance of seeking counsel from people who are patient and who understand God sometimes takes years to heal troubled areas in our marriages and in our personal lives. And I have to accept I may not see complete healing in my spouse (or myself) this side of heaven.

As I think of God having patience with me and my need to have patience with my husband, I recall sin areas in my life I've battled since childhood—overeating, being critical, having a negative attitude and more. I still haven't conquered them completely. Often I feel convinced Randy's sins are worse than mine. As I draw close to God, I discover He doesn't see it that way.

Chapter 9

While I Am Waiting

Years ago I asked myself this question: *So what do I do while I wait?* Once I decided, "I'm willing to wait," I needed to move on to actions which bring glory to God and keep my love for my husband alive. In the past I nagged, compared, complained, and schemed. Then I learned to concentrate on the following while I waited for God to "please do something!" in my husband's life.

#1 Keep a journal.
#2 Pray without ceasing.
#3 Let God heal my wounds.
#4 Develop a grateful heart.
#5 Keep my eyes on the Lord.

1 Keep a journal.

I discovered I needed to avoid allowing my journal to be a place where I keep a record of my husband's faults. Instead I write down what my husband does right. Also, I let my journal be where I cry out to God and write down how He intervenes. I also write about God's goodness and grace.

The next four suggestions for what God wanted me to do while I waited I worked out in my journal.

#2 Pray Without Ceasing

Too often when I faced hard times in my marriage, I failed to pray or I aborted my prayer life when it seemed "nothing's happening."

One day after spending weeks praying about a certain sin area in my husband's life, I decided to talk to him about it. The talk soon turned into a fight. What Randy said next showed me that my prayers were helping, and I should have chosen silence and continued to wait:

"Why did you bring this up? God was already dealing with me in this area in recent days."

#3 Let God Heal My Wounds

Instead of time spent in a pursuit of my healing from God, I spent much time scheming to try to get my husband healed. As I allow God to heal my wounds, I determine to feel my pain and work through it. When I remain in pain over something my husband did days, weeks, months or even years ago, I see only his faults and need for transformation

I discovered I remained unhealed from various traumas in my childhood, and often what Randy said or did triggered pain. Through the help of a counselor, prayer, and much time in the Word, God brought me tremendous healing of childhood hurts, which helped me to love Randy.

#4 Develop a Grateful Heart.

I discovered an excellent way for me to check my attitude: Ask, "Am I giving thanks as I wait for the Lord to finish His work in Randy, in our marriage, and in me?"

Often I meet a wife who can't think of one good thing about the man she married. When I meet her husband, I immediately see character qualities I respect. That dark place where I can't see one good thing in my man is somewhere I've been too, but then I look at my husband through the eyes of others who love him, or through the Lord's eyes, and I see God-given beauty in him. That's because I can take his good qualities for granted—like his sense of humor, his compassion, his being affectionate, his being a hard worker and excellent provider, his high intelligence and superior problem-solving skills. And the list goes on.

Gratitude can transform a negative attitude toward my husband in a way nothing else can. I thank God for the small things too. I thank God Randy fixed the broken light switch recently without me even asking him to. It helps my attitude to speak my gratitude out loud to the Lord, to my husband and to others.

#5 Keep My Eyes on The Lord.

Years ago a friend urged me to: "Glance at your problems, and keep your eyes on the Lord." How often I magnified marriage problems and made my wait time excruciating. Instead I learned to embrace magnifying the Lord. "I will praise the name of God with song and magnify Him with thanksgiving" (Psalm 69:30 AMP). I learned when I magnify my marriage problems, I cannot magnify the Lord. One way to magnify the Lord is to "worship in the waiting"—a saying I heard years ago.

This verse about focusing on the Lord has meant so much

to me during my waiting times in marriage: "Fixing our eyes on Jesus, the pioneer and perfecter of faith" (Hebrews 12:2). As I keep my eyes on the Lord, I move from comparing and complaining.

When I keep my eyes on the Lord and seek Him, He presents to me the big picture. Holding to God's perspective and what He desires rather than what I want, keeps me believing God is bringing good out of the trials in our marriage.

Cooperating With the Lord

As I cooperate with Him, God draws me closer to Himself and makes me more like Christ. He shows me my willingness to wait in my marriage is a picture of God's patience with His children.

Years ago I caught Randy looking at porn when I thought he conquered the problem for good—one of many relapses. In the past I screamed and yelled and had weeks-long pity parties. This time instead of saying anything I went into the bathroom and cried out to God. Lord, please speak to me about this problem in our marriage, I prayed. God gave me Psalm 62:1 "For God alone my soul waits in silence; from Him comes my salvation" (AMP). I didn't say a word to Randy about it, but kept my focus on the Lord. Soon after, he went to counseling and was able to make great strides in conquering the problem.

Blessings come as I determine to be a patient wife. After years of waiting, one thing that's true is this: it's been worth the wait.

Lord, You are a patient God, and I know you desire I be a patient wife. Help me to wait on You. In Jesus' name I pray. Amen

Part V

A Passion for Compassion

Love is…kind. —1 Corinthians 13:4

Compassion is the antitoxin of the soul. —Eric Hoffer

Chapter 10

Lord, Help Me Be Kind

"Kind = affectionate, loving, characterized by sympathy or forbearance, agreeable; considerate, compassionate, concerned, helpful, thoughtful," I read in my dictionary. In the definition of "kind," I feel most drawn to the word "compassionate." This verse comes to mind, "...our God is full of compassion" (Psalm 116:5). In the midst of my battle with showing compassion toward my husband, I prayed, "Lord, help me to be full of compassion, like You."

A Turning Point

One turning point in my marriage in regard to compassion came the day our pastor preached a sermon about the Good Samaritan. That day the Lord spoke this to me: "Your husband is that wounded man on the side of the road."

Although Randy acted macho and pretended he had everything together, I knew how deep wounds of his childhood affected relationships with the opposite sex as well as his friendships.

I read in Luke 10:30 that a man "was attacked by robbers," and immediately I thought of Satan, the thief, and his demons.

Those robbers in the story, "stripped him of his clothes, beat him and went away, leaving him half dead."

In verse 31, I read that a priest came by, but "when he saw the man, he passed by on the other side." A Levite did the same (verse 32). I realized as I read these verses that like they did, I sometimes adopted a righteous, holier-than-thou attitude—to create an emotional distance between my husband and me so as not to look at his wounds. I too often thought, *he must have done something to deserve or to cause those wounds.*

God wants me to imitate the Samaritan in this story who, "when he saw him" (he came close enough to look; the others only saw him from a distance), "he took pity on him. He went to him and bandaged his wounds, pouring on oil and wine." (verses 33-34) In the Scripture oil symbolizes the Holy Spirit and wine represents the blood of Jesus. My goal is to have the compassion of the Holy Spirit and the forgiveness of Jesus.

Keys to Compassion

Although I wanted to imitate the good Samaritan, a part of me remained angry because out of my husband's woundedness came betrayals and unkindness toward me. What I read in *Every Heart Restored* by Brenda Stoeker (Waterbrook Press 2004, 2010) helped. "Sure, his sin is betraying and crushing you, but it is also revealing his deeper wounds and addictions below the surface. He's not just a straying husband but a brother lost in the futility of his thinking and now corrupted by his deceitful desires. It's not just about you."

She goes on to say, "The way I came to view things, I was not just Fred's wife…I was also his good Samaritan, compelled by my love to dress his wounds, and also his friend, taking on the 'iron sharpens iron' role described in Proverbs 27:17…Yes, sparks can fly when iron sharpens iron, but the results sought should always be mutual healing..." Brenda continues: "...a 'dressing his wound' mind-set is crucial to a wife's approach to any of her husband's sins, whether it's anger or porn." (pages 158-159)

As I became compassionate, I grew in my desire to get to know Randy and his wounds. His abandonment issues became obvious. When the children were younger he said, "Every woman in my life abandoned me—except for you." I thought of his mom's and sister's abandonment through mental illness and never fulfilling the roles of mom or sister to him again after their severe breakdowns. I thought of a trusted female employee who embezzled $200,000 from his business. I thought of the girlfriend before me who wrote him a "Dear John," letter while he served away from home in the Marine Corps and awaited orders, possibly to Viet Nam. (Through a miracle, his orders kept him on his base stateside.)

I can't force my husband to release the effects of trauma, but I can keep from traumatizing him further. Wounded by a hypercritical, controlling mother, his trauma increases if I focus on criticizing him.

Because of Randy's unresolved trauma, he often unintentionally passes trauma along to me through behaviors to deal with his pain which hurt me, i.e., porn, anger and actions which shut me out of his life, such as excessive time spent in front of the TV or on the computer. But God promises to heal my broken heart and bind up my wounds. (See Psalm 147:3.) Even if Randy doesn't allow God to heal his broken heart and bind up his wounds, God will do both of these for me. However, in recent months Randy invited God to heal these wounds, and I'm overwhelmed with joy.

Chapter 11

Dealing With Compassion Fatigue

Even as I learned compassion, I discovered I sometimes become weary of caring. A term I found in a book described my condition: compassion fatigue. As I prayed for God to help me work through my fatigue, He gave me these instructions:

#1 Stop taking things personally.

A while ago I asked a friend for a tip about marriage to share with others. She said, "Don't take things personally."

When caught up in my own emotions, I easily feel wounded and take rejections personally.

When in a godly frame of mind, instead of the "it's all about me," mindset, my heart becomes overwhelmed with compassion for my husband when he lashes out in anger. I think how hurt he must feel to overreact like he does. Instead of the repeated question of, *How could he treat me like this?* I pray, *Lord, please intervene in his life and empower me to treat him kindly—even when he's unable to do that for me at this moment.*

I found my marriage more peaceful as I learned to let go of this personal effrontery frame of mind. I obsess less and experience more empathy and compassion.

As I concentrate on compassion, I sense the depths of God's love for me, His compassion, toward me and how far He's brought me. When I express my love for God through compassion, it passes along His love to Randy, especially when it seems he doesn't deserve it. None of us deserves it. That's what makes God's love so amazing.

#2 See From God's Perspective

I learned the more I draw close to God, the more compassion I feel for my husband. When I go to the Lord in prayer for our marriage or for my husband. I sometimes enter the prayer time full of anger and even a sense of revenge, but by the time I leave, compassion for my husband replaces my frustration, because my Lord, who knows Randy better than I do, loves him in spite of his actions and urges me to do the same.

As I study the Word to discover how to be kinder, the "least of these" verses arise as vital. Even when I think, "He's the worst husband in the world," God still wants me to show compassion. I read in Matthew 25: "Then the righteous will answer him, 'Lord, when did we see you hungry and feed you, or thirsty and give you something to drink? When did we see you a stranger and invite you in, or needing clothes and clothe you? When did we see you sick or in prison and go to visit you? The King will reply, 'Truly I tell you, whatever you did for one of the least of these brothers and sisters of mine, you did for me.'" (verses 37-40) When we see our spouses as "least," and remain kind, we can think of doing it as unto Jesus.

As I seek God and ask for His kindness—His compassion—to flow through me, He shows me Randy's issue with masculinity. One day Randy revealed he felt so negative toward his mom because "she emasculated my father through her controlling ways." I remembered Randy talked often of his mother's attempts to

49

control him as well, and I felt he failed to finish the sentence: "and she tried to emasculate me."

When I engage in control instead of compassion, I rob my husband of his sense of manhood. His negative behaviors center on what some worldly men do to feel manly—anger, profanity, porn, along with others—exactly what his mother told him not to do. For years his mind held him in a trap fueled by a lie which he sometimes voiced: if I quit these behaviors, I'm not a man, and I've let her control me.

As I drew near to the Lord, I also learned Randy isn't my enemy. Satan is. Too often I block compassion because I see my husband as my enemy. Yet even if I see him as such, the Word commands me to love my enemies, so I still don't remain excuseless. "But love your enemies, do good to them…" (Luke 6:35).

God's perspective helped me let go of these C's which prevent compassion: comparison, criticism, condemnation, and control.

#3 Let Go of Judging

One day I wondered, "What is the opposite of compassion?" This is what I found in my dictionary: "Callousness, judgment, cruelty."

I saw in me a callous attitude when my husband was suffering and lashed out in the midst. At those times I saw only my own pain. I tended to judge why he did what he did, and usually ended up with, "He does this just to hurt me."

As I matured and let God speak to me, I saw it as untrue, but my counselor also gave me a truth, "Emma, it doesn't matter who your husband was married to. He would use these same coping mechanisms to deal with the pain in his life."

Another male counselor I consulted expressed such tender compassion for my husband's struggles, it was contagious. He urged me to invite kindly instead of demand—definitely a more compassionate way to deal with marriage problems.

John Fischer explains about judging in the book, *12 Steps for the Recovering Pharisee (like me)* (Bethany House Publishers, 2000) "The act of judging gives us a subjective means of affirming ourselves. No matter what I've done or how bad I am, I can always comfort myself by finding someone out there who is 'worse' than I am." (page 16) I hate to say my husband often fit that description.

It's imperative to avoid judging my husband. When I wrongly judge the motives behind my husband's actions, my perspective of him becomes different than God's, and I fall into Satan's trap of judging. I learned God knows his heart, his hurts, and his motives. I realized as a child I also judged my parent's motives. In every area of my life, judgment leads to cruel words and walls, which cut off compassion.

If I surround myself with other bitter wives, we sink deeper into callousness and judging our husbands, rather than exhibiting compassion toward them. When I spend time with other compassionate wives, I avoid judging and grow in compassion.

Chapter 12

Compassion: A Gift From God

While with a group of women one day, I spoke of issues in my husband's life and how God taught me to have compassion. I discovered my "audience" consisted of bitter ex-wives. They put me down for my passion for compassion. One woman said, "I'm more the pack-my-bags-and-leave" kind of wife. She admitted to it twice so far. To her, it seemed unusual for me to show compassion toward someone who hurt me, even though she professed Christianity and attended church regularly.

I told her at times I too felt the pack-my-bags urge, but when it came, God gave me this prayer to say: "Lord, when I want to run away, give me strength to stay and pray."

When He Doesn't Want To Be Healed

I believe in God's power to heal. One of the main problems in our marriage arose when I jumped in with both feet to deal with pains and hurts from my past. Unfortunately, my husband does not possess fervor for that pursuit. One day he affirmed it when a speaker appeared on a television program. She said we need to bring to our marriage our own best selves. Randy said,

"You've done that, and I haven't." *What a moment of insight*, I thought, since he often denied his issues. But instead of hate toward my husband for his lack of desire to be healed —actually his terror of the process—I can become a part of the healing process.

I see my husband as the wounded man on the side of the road, but too often I sense he resists any actions I make to move him toward a place of healing. But yet God does not want me to stop my attempts. And some days he does respond, and I praise God for that.

True Compassion

One friend's statement tempted me away from compassion when she said, "I'm sick of forgiving." Often, I become worn out when I care about Randy when he doesn't seem to care about himself or me. I sink into despair when I constantly show compassion for him when he expresses no compassion for me.

When I move back to a distorted view of marriage, I think I can show compassion only if I receive compassion first. The word "compassionate" contains the word "passion." Passion means more than to be fired up or enthusiastic. In the phrase "the passion of the Christ," the title of a movie, passion also signifies suffering. To show compassion toward my husband means a willingness to suffer for his sake, the opposite concept to what our culture teaches. But this theme permeates Scripture. 1 Peter 4:13 spells it out: "But rejoice inasmuch as you participate in the sufferings of Christ, so that you may be overjoyed when his glory is revealed." Whenever I exhibit true compassion toward others, and it involves suffering, I share in Christ's suffering.

Compassion does not include an open door to allow my husband to tyrannize or abuse me. I need to set boundaries. But when Randy does something mean, God wants me to see it from His perspective rather than as an attack on me. Instead of wallowing in self-pity, I go to the Lord and ask, "God, how should I respond?" His answer always involves love—not revenge.

One wife kept her compassion level up when she wrote a love letter to her husband every day when they separated because of his sexual addiction. She didn't send the letters, but they kept her from losing compassion for her husband. Eventually he came home and made great progress in his healing.

It helps me to keep in mind that compassion doesn't come naturally to me. It comes from the Lord as a supernatural gift. The closer I move toward Him, the more compassion I show toward my husband.

God Can Resurrect Compassion

Even if my compassion for my husband seems dead and kindness toward him seems wrong, God desires to resurrect the compassion in my heart. I celebrate the fact He does it again and again. The demonstration of kindness when it seems Randy doesn't deserve it, works miracles in my marriage. It demonstrates exactly what God did for me. But in the end, even if my husband doesn't notice my kindness, God certainly does.

Lord, thank You for Your compassion for me. Give me a willing heart to be kind to my husband even when he's not kind to me. Remind me when I do that, I bring honor to You, and I will reap what I sow. In Jesus' name I pray. Amen.

Part VI

Learning Contentment

Love...does not envy. —1 Corinthians 13:4

Contentment is not the fulfillment of what you want,
but the realization of how much you already have.
—Source unknown.

Chapter 13

Let Go of Marriage Envy

"Surprise!" we shouted as Irene walked through the door. She shrieked with joy as she looked around the room at the elegant restaurant. Tears came to her eyes as she greeted the 30 friends gathered there. Irene hugged her husband, who arranged her 65th birthday gathering, and exclaimed, "Thank you. Thank you."

How wonderful that her husband would honor her in this way, I thought.

My husband would never do this for me, came my next thought. I felt myself start to slide down the same slippery slope which plagued me too many times before in our 36-year marriage. A knot formed in my stomach. The excellent food suddenly tasted foul. *God, please help me.*

I called out to the Lord early that day, which helped protect me from a flare-up of a disease which, otherwise, might begin to eat away at my heart. Left unchecked, this ailment carries the potential to destroy a marriage.

Called marriage envy, the symptoms center around jealousy of those with what I perceive as an easier, more loving or more godly husband than mine. Even excellent marriages sometimes fall prey to this deadly affliction. I discovered four ways which helped me overcome marriage envy, so I could find contentment with my own husband.

#1 Avoid Comparisons

Comparisons lead to self-pity, harsh criticisms, and withdrawal from my spouse. An innocent comment from another wife sometimes starts the comparison ball rolling. "My husband and I never fight" or "I'm so thankful for my godly husband." Envying them hurts my love for them and for my husband.

I noticed when I compare, I tend to measure another husband's strengths against my husband's weaknesses. Do I want Randy to do so with other wives? Certainly not.

God showed me when I compare, I cannot see the whole picture. Years ago, with my focus riveted on this destructive pursuit, He opened my eyes.

"Randy doesn't help around the house the way Tracy's husband does," I moaned often.

Then I saw the reason. My friend's husband's help centered on his perfectionism. He criticized her housekeeping and redid what she already cleaned.

On another occasion, I compared my husband's feeble romantic gestures to the man who frequently gave his wife flowers. Later, the wife told me of her husband's affairs and added, "those were guilt flowers."

Another man, a member of our church, helped with the children more than Randy did. God showed me his attitude toward his wife: "She's an incompetent mother." Sadly, all three of these marriages ended in divorce.

God gave me alternatives when tempted to compare and think "My husband doesn't care like hers does…" First, I confess my comparisons as sin. Then I count my blessings. They may be different than other wives' blessings, but they remain too many to count.

#2 Develop An Attitude of Gratitude

I include at least one thank you a day during my prayer time. I start with "Thank You, Lord, for Randy and for our marriage." Then I recall a recent kindness I can be thankful for such as, "Thank You that Randy worked in the yard, and it looks great." Later, I pass these thank yous along to Randy verbally and in cards and notes. Saying "thank you" can do much to bring contentment to my heart.

Lately, I learned to say spontaneously to my husband, "Thank you for loving me" and then adding something, i.e., "by handling our finances so well," or "by not swearing in my presence." Instead of an angry proclamation that Randy doesn't love me perfectly, I celebrate the way he shows me he loves me and considers me his lifelong best friend and how he doesn't give up on me when I'm the one who's difficult to live with. Oh, how I cringe when I think of the days when I suffered with severe PMS.

Part of my gratitude must also go to God. One day, as I prayed in the prayer room at our church, I wrote in the anonymous prayer journal there at a point when I felt weary of problems in our relationship.

"I've been praying the same prayers for over thirty years, and nothing has changed," I complained in writing.

God then showed me the changes He wrought in my husband, but not just the quick, sweeping, grand changes I wanted. So, instead of saying "thank You, Lord" when I saw a change, my past attitude became, "That's not enough." Contentment comes when I open my eyes to how Randy's transformation comes over time—even if not in my time table.

#3 Gain a Godly Perspective

God showed me my contentment must remain based on Him, not on what my husband says or does. When I keep my eyes on the Lord, He fills me with joy at who He is and all He does in and through Randy and me. When I move my focus away from how I want the marriage someone else has, and maintain a godly perspective, I see God at work in our marriage.

What one wife said at a women's retreat inspired me: "Marriage is not all about me and my happiness. It is about God and what He wants to do in me and through me."

As I pray for God's perspective, I sometimes reach the point where I truly praise God for problems in our marriage. The difficulties we faced together as a couple, caused my love for my husband and my dependence on the Lord to grow deeper.

Even though trials threaten to rob me of contentment, I still rest in the fact God uses trials to grow me and transform me into a more loving wife.

#4 Believe Contentment Is Possible

Contentment does not come naturally to human beings. Paul says this about the subject: "...I have *learned* to be content [and self-sufficient through Christ, satisfied to the point where I am not disturbed or uneasy] regardless of my circumstances" (Philippians 4:11 AMP-- emphasis mine).

Since Paul made this statement while in prison, even if my marriage feels like some sort of prison, I too can achieve contentment.

Psalm 23:1, with a little twist I added, helps me: "The Lord is my Shepherd, I shall not want any other husband or any other life than the one He has so graciously given to me..."

As I learned to find contentment, I stopped using up energy longing for what others experience, and instead use it for working on my relationship with my husband.

My husband loves when I'm a contented wife who lets it show. This helps bring peace to our home and serves as a key to our love-for-a-lifetime lasting marriage.

Chapter 14

Let Go of Complaining

Complaints begin with an attitude of *Surely I deserve better than this.* But according to the Word, God gives me much more than I deserve. When I focus on the wonder of God's grace, I see so much to thank Him for, especially that He loves me—even when it seems my husband doesn't.

The less I whine about the negative aspects of my life and my marriage, the more clearly I see the positives, which I tend to take for granted. If I feel I must complain, I take my complaints to God. He doesn't feel overburdened—like my friends and family often do—when I moan to Him. My Lord always listens objectively—and then opens my eyes to see my world from His perspective. He brings my life into focus as He reminds me of the many times He worked His best when my life languished at its worst.

These days, when I ask God how to fully receive His peace and contentment, He shows me that when I speak positive words about my marriage, it fuels contentment. I'm praying for grace to live out Philippians 2:14-16. "Do everything without grumbling or arguing, so that you may become blameless and pure, 'children of God without fault in a warped and crooked generation.' Then you will shine among them like stars in the sky as you hold firmly to the word of life...."

Complaints about my marriage bring about a certain kind of death in my spirit and in the spirits of those around me. It works to kill my passion for God, my purpose in God, and my perspective from God. Groaning sets up a dam to stop the flow of peace.

Attention Deficit Disorder and Contentment

When I discovered I suffered from ADD—Attention Deficit Disorder, I realized it kept me from feeling loved and content with Randy's love. Not the same disorder from which children suffer, mine contains a different spin. I didn't get enough attention as a child, so for years I looked to Randy to give me extra attention to make up for my childhood lack, and I complained often when he didn't.

Unfortunately, it came across as controlling, which caused Randy to withdraw. When he did show me attention, no matter how much he gave me, it never seemed enough.

When I called out to the Lord about this, He showed me His way: Give Randy attention; give extra attention to *his* needs. He reminded me that, in marriage and in our Christian lives, we reap what we sow. (See Galatians 6:7). A friend recently reminded me that the reaping comes in God's timing, not ours.

Now that Randy is retired, he gives me attention. I realize when he was employed, he focused more on his career and dealing with its stress, which often caused him to withdraw.

Chapter 15

Letting Go of Discontent

One day, I felt envious of a lady who seemed to suffer minimally in her marriage. *Lord, it's not fair,* I thought. But then I looked more closely at her life. A Christian, but not walking close to God, she battled worldliness and ungodliness. I saw the suffering in my marriage purged me from these same issues. I learned to thank God for any suffering and to focus on contentment that God knows what He's doing. He chose marriage to transform me. In other people's lives he chooses other avenues.

I stopped attending a women's Bible study for a while because the leader kept calling her husband her "sweetheart" whenever she referred to him. I felt she rubbed salt in my wounds, and the message I heard was, "I'm blessed with a wonderful husband nah nah nah nah nah nah." Later I brought it up to her, and I realized, after our conversation, that her marriage lacked, but by calling her husband "sweetheart" in front of others, it kept her attitude in the right place. It helped her retain her sense of contentment.

The Myth of Compatibility

As I write this, a spokesman on the TV hawks the dating service he started. He uses the words, "soul mate," and because it seems that so often Randy doesn't understand me, I've thought "he isn't my soul mate, and I can't be content, because we're not compatible." I discovered even married people go on these dating sites to look for people they can call their "soul mates."

It took me years to reach the point of being content that God uses our lack of compatibility in certain areas to cause us to become more like Him. I'm so glad Jesus didn't desert His mission on this earth with the excuse of "I just don't feel compatible with those people."

I like what Leo Tolstoy wrote about the subject: "What counts in making a happy marriage is not so much how compatible you are but how you deal with incompatibility."

Receiving Joy from the Lord

Sometimes I ask myself, "Is this all there is to marriage?" If I don't receive all God has for me, it's not because of my husband. He can't keep me from receiving joy from the Lord; He can't prevent me from feeling happy.

Other times I miss the good aspects in my marriage and the sense of contentment I need because I hold back. I fail in my honesty about what I think and feel. I let fear rule the day.

At the luncheon I mentioned earlier, I confessed to a friend sitting next to me that I was battling looking at other people's marriages and lives with thoughts like, "Boy, wouldn't I like to have a life like that?" Then she said something which surprised me, "Emma, there are so many people who look at your life and say the same thing."

She was right. Not long ago I found a quote that goes along with that: "The things you take for granted someone else is praying for."

I learn contentment as I lean on the Lord. That's what I need to do a lot more–lean on and learn from Him.

Lord, I praise You that I can learn contentment. Let me communicate contentment to my husband even when things aren't as I want them to be. In Jesus' name I pray. Amen.

Part VII

Humility—The Key to A Happily Ever After Marriage

"Love… does not boast, it is not proud."
—1 Corinthians 13:4

If you plan to build a tall house of virtues, you must first lay deep foundations of humility. —Augustine

Chapter 16

Letting Go of Pride

Pride says:	Humility Says:
I'm never supposed to hurt.	God, use this pain for Your glory.
Lord, this is what You must do.	Lord, I submit. Tell me what to do.
I must get my husband to repent.	Lord, I repent of my wicked ways.
His sin is worse than mine.	Have mercy on me, a sinner. Luke 18:13
Let me tell him a thing or two.	Lord, what do You have to say to me?
My happiness is my #1 concern.	What can I do to make him happy and to please You, Lord?
It's my job to change my husband.	Lord, I entrust my husband to You.
Lord, You've got to change him.	Lord, please change me.

I can't take this anymore.	I can do all this through him who gives me strength.. Philippians 4:13
Lord, can't you see what he's doing?	Search me, God...Psalm 139:23
I'm trying to hold things together.	...in him all things hold together. Col 1:17
There's no help for us.	God is...an ever-present help...Ps 46:1
Lord, I can't forgive him.	Lord, give me the grace to forgive him as You forgave me.

I created this chart for a women's retreat where I spoke about humility in marriage. When the director of the conference asked me for the title of the talk, I said, "Am I A Humble Wife?"

"Emma, we can't go with that title," she insisted.

She felt most women wouldn't admit to a pride problem.

I prayed, and this title popped into my mind: "The Key To A Happily-Ever-After Marriage." The room filled up. Only when they settled in their seats did I let them know the subject of our time together centered on humility, a vital component of happy marriages.

After the class, a woman stopped me and said, "I've been married for 31 years, and I learned more today about marriage in your class than I have throughout my entire married life."

The enemy wants to keep us blind to our pride problems.

Pride and My View of Sin

God revealed an aspect of my pride issue when He pointed out my mixed-up view of sin. My sins—a critical, judgmental attitude for example—seemed small and harmless to me compared to Randy's temper or his excessive time in front of the television and computer screens, rather than with the children and me.

God showed me the error of this and how much pride I hid in my heart, when I read Jesus' words in Matthew 7:5: "You hypocrite, first take the plank out of your own eye, and then you will see clearly to remove the speck from your brother's eye."

When I let God expose my motives and attitudes in the light of His Word, my sins always appear like planks, while Randy's grow smaller in comparison. God wants me to deal with *my* own sin problems.

Watch Your Mouth

While in the Marines and as a construction worker, Randy perfected the "art" of profanity. Too often he let loose a string of swear words. I worried about its negative effect on our children, particularly when they uttered a curse word. I also often felt sorry for myself for the burden of life with a man who couldn't control his use of swear words around me.

One day I prayed haughtily, "Lord, deliver him from this evil habit" after my repeated reprimands failed. But then the Holy Spirit spoke to me, *What about* your *mouth?* Suddenly these words came to mind—criticism, complaints, gossip. I cringed when I realized our children picked up these sinful habits as well. The truth hit me: My use of words proved no better than my husband's. Pride blinded me to that fact.

Partners in the battle against sin.

As God humbles me, I see that Randy and I stand as equals. We each battle to overcome sinful habits in our lives. I feel close to my husband when we help each other in an atmosphere of love, not condemnation.

In her book *Every Heart Restored*, Brenda Stoeker (Waterbrook Press, 2004, 2010) urges wives: "Pray, too, for humility. Humility makes forgiveness possible and opens the door to oneness. God is perfectly capable of dealing with your husband in His time once you've laid down your arms and allowed Him to take the center of your marriage. Your humility releases an opportunity for victory in your life." (page 127)

My prideful attitude sometimes blocked the way for change, and placed a dam on the flow of love from my heart to Randy. When pride rules my heart, I become blind to how regularly change takes place in Randy's heart and life.

Chapter 17

Marriage—God's Tool to Humble Me

I'm convinced marriage works as one of God's main tools to humble us. When Randy's worst behavior exposes the worst in me, I must humble myself enough to go to God and repent. Then I ask Him to give me a more humble attitude—to make me more like Jesus. God shows me that just because Randy behaves in a sinful manner does not excuse my ungodly response.

When I battle a prideful attitude, a slow read of Philippians 2:5-8 helps. The beauty of Christ's humility makes me want to cry. How I long to be humble like him. What a difference deep humility could make in our marriage and in every one of my relationships. "Have this same attitude in yourselves which was in Christ Jesus: [look to Him as your example in selfless humility:] ... (verse 2 AMP)

A New View of Humility

The Word instructs me to consider others better than myself. (See Philippians 2:3). Not long ago someone told me of a new way to look at the verse. This friend said to add this little phrase to better understand. "If I had been through all they have been through, I could not have handled it better."

I think of my husband and the two most influential women in his life who suffered from severe mental illness. How would I deal with men if all the males closest to me in my childhood proved unstable, unreliable, over-emotional and delusional? He has actually done exceptionally well, considering all He went through.

God Resists Me When I'm Proud

Many times when I realized how filled with pride I became, I wondered what blessings I missed because of it. When I cried out for help and none seemed to come, I realized I could blame my full-of-demands, prideful, attitude.

The book, *The Faith Which Overcomes* by Dwight L. Moody, (published by The Book Society for the Circulation of Biblical Literature, London, England) written way back in 1750, contains truths which still shine bright today: "I believe that if we are humble enough we shall be sure to get a great blessing. After all, I think that more depends on us than upon the Lord; because He is always ready to give a blessing and give it freely, but we are not always in a position to receive it. He always blesses the humble; and, if we can get down in the dust before Him, no one will go away disappointed."(Page 82)

After Pride Comes A Fall

The Word promises this: "Pride goeth before destruction, and an haughty spirit before a fall" (Proverbs 16:18 KJV).

One day I pridefully reprimanded my husband because he yelled at our granddaughter. My attitude communicated, "I will not let you do that," and underneath, "I'm so much better than you; I would never yell at her like that."

Later that day, my granddaughter sassed me, and I lost my temper and yelled at her even louder than he did—in my husband's presence. I fell into the same behavior for which I corrected my husband—because of pride.

Pride Can Block Receiving Love

Pride keeps me from receiving the love my husband offers me. If I demand my husband love me in a certain way (to demand always involves pride), and then he refuses, I become blind to all the ways he does love me. I went through this in my relationship with the Lord as well. The more humble I become, the more my heart opens to notice and receive all God has for me and to notice how my husband loves me—even if he fails to do it in the perfect way I desire.

Perfectionism and Pride

Sometimes perfectionism stands at the root of my pride problem. Too often I mourned the shattered dream of a perfect marriage. Though my marriage remains less than perfect when compared to my ideal, God showed me something better: I can seek a perfect heart toward Him—a humble, teachable heart.

Back when perfectionism caught me in its trap, I felt good about my ability to follow certain rules of Christianity, while my husband failed at them. I knew lots of Bible verses, and I recited them to him repeatedly. Over time, I learned some called this spiritual abuse. Although I often quoted Scriptures to friends, and they received them eagerly, when my spouse resides in a position of unbelief or rebellion, to assault him with the Bible displeases both him and God.

This verse stopped me from the practice of blows to my husband with Scripture verses: "Wives, in the same way submit yourselves to your own husbands so that, if any of them do not believe the word, they may be won over without words (God showed me it includes words from the Bible) by the behavior of their wives" (1 Peter 3:1).

Chapter 18

More Aspects of Humility

I learned a humble wife dedicates herself to service. I think of Jesus when He washed the disciples' feet and called them to be servants. (See John 13:1-17). Too often I want my husband and even God to serve me. The enemy convinces me my importance supersedes all others. I hurt to think how many times I still fall into that trap. When it happened weeks ago, God brought it to my attention when He whispered, "Emma, at the center of this most recent conflict resides this false belief: I am better than Randy."

Our pastor said not long ago, "The happiest people are those who serve. The most miserable person is the self-absorbed." He added, "The culture teaches us to be self-absorbed." I confess in our marriage me, me, me often takes over in place of what I can do to serve Randy.

To Die To Self and Humility

I remember a day years ago which impacted me greatly. As I drove home from a session with my counselor, I focused on how messed up I felt in my relationships because of traumas from my past, which still wreaked havoc in my thought life.

"I want to die," thoughts invaded my mind. I began to review methods of suicide and whether I should consider the option since God refused to answer my pleas to "Take me home."

Then a whisper came, "I want you to die."

Was that from the enemy? But then I realized the Lord longed for me to understand a concept in the Bible—the need to die to self—to my will and to my way. My misery at that time overwhelmed me because I held to self-protection, self-pity, self-absorption, and the list went on—all issues associated with pride.

In 1 Corinthians 15:31 Paul states, "I die daily [I face death and die to self" (AMP).

As I ask the Lord to help me die to myself, Jesus' words in Matthew 16:24 also come to mind: "'Whoever wants to be my disciple must deny themselves and take up their cross and follow me.'"

Hardened Hearts

Hardened hearts and pride go together. In Matthew 19:8 Jesus said to people who asked him about divorce: "'Because your hearts were hard and stubborn Moses permitted you to divorce your wives; but from the beginning it has not been this way" (AMP). In this verse I see another word which goes along with pride: stubbornness.

God desires to talk to me about how to love my husband and how I fail to do so, but a hardened heart caused by pride keeps me deaf. Humility opens up my spiritual ears. When I give in to deafness to God's voice, pride tells me all the problems in our marriage fall with Randy. As humility takes hold of my heart, God shows me my part in our marriage problems. God honors my repeated prayer: "Lord, soften my heart."

Deal with Self-pity

As I ask the Lord to deliver me from pride, I discover one sure sign of a pride is self-pity. I admitted I gave in to self-pity, but for a long time failed to tie it to pride. Then I read this quote by Oswald Chambers in *My Utmost For His Highest*. "No sin is worse than the sin of self-pity because it obliterates God and puts self-interest on the throne."

When I let go of self-pity fueled by pride, I see how God blesses me richly.

Rest and Humility

When I rest in the Lord, I discover humility. Jesus said in Matthew 11:28-30: "Come to me, all you who are weary and burdened, and I will give you rest. Take my yoke upon you and learn from me, for I am gentle and humble in heart, and you will find rest for your souls. For my yoke is easy and my burden is light." Wow! Rest, easy, light. I like those words, and I receive.

Pride and attempts to run the show called "my marriage" wear me out. When I embrace humility, I receive the bonus of God's rest.

Lord, empower me to be humble enough to receive Your grace to make it through hard times. Humble me enough to let me see my husband as You see him and to love Him as You do. In Jesus' precious name I pray. Amen.

Part VIII

The ABCs of Respect

It (love) is not rude. —1 Corinthians 13:5 AMP

If women could learn to understand that respect is a man's native tongue, that it absolutely heals his heart and ministers to him like nothing else, it would make the biggest difference in the world. —unknown

Chapter 19

Discovering My Disrespect

One day I decided to make a list for Randy titled: "Ways Randy is too harsh." My list contained eleven items, but could be condensed to, "Randy shows harshness when his words hurt rather than encourage and when his attitude exudes superiority."

After I read my list, I felt certain Randy would understand my needs completely, embrace me, and whisper sweet words in my ear like he did when we first fell in love. Just as I determined to give him my list, I remembered the start of a recent skirmish.

Randy: "What did you do with my pliers?"

Me: "I didn't touch them. You always accuse me of taking your things."

Randy (who notices I make no move to get up from my chair). "Help me find them. Now!"

Me: "Find them yourself. You're the one who lost them."

For the first time, I noticed my side of the conversation. I realized I, and not just Randy, ignored needs. I failed to consider Randy's need for respect.

Although I knew Colossians 3:19: "Husbands, love your wives and do not be harsh with them," somehow I overlooked Ephesians 5:33: "...the wife must respect her husband."

Underneath these petty exchanges, each of us cried out—me for love and Randy for respect. So, before I gave Randy my list, I asked him to make a list of "Ways Emma Does Not Respect Me." Then we exchanged lists.

Randy handled my list graciously and expressed surprise at some of the items I listed. Randy's list proved longer than I expected and included issues like "tries to dominate, argues, shows no appreciation, contradicts me, lectures me, accuses me, refuses to listen, and presumes to know me better than I know myself."

We took our negative lists and condensed them into positive lists. I wrote "Ways Randy Can Show Me Tenderness": speak gently even when he's frustrated, comfort me when I get upset, and make eye contact when I speak.

His list included: express appreciation, notice his accomplishments, and listen to him. I noticed a similarity on each list: become better listeners.

These two lists brought increased understanding and made our lives more peaceful, but we can occasionally fall into temptation and go back to our old habits. When Randy ignores tenderness, I want to say, "Hey, what about the list?" But I know the purpose of the list. To benefit him, not me—to help him understand me. The list I need to focus on now: how to show him respect.

When I show respect for my husband—even when I don't feel like it or when I think he doesn't deserve it—I'm demonstrating mature, lasting love, evidenced when I respond the right way. Love means meeting his needs, even when my needs go unmet.

Let Go of Treating Him Like A Child

Part of the disrespect which bound me for years showed up when I treated Randy like a child. Instead of a respectful wife—especially during times of conflicts, when he handled stress badly, or got caught up in sins which crushed me and hurt our marriage—I resorted to the controlling, correcting mother role. I withheld respect as a mother withholds candy from a naughty child.

Over time and after many mistakes, I learned when my husband acts like a child not to act as a mother and scold him. This action damaged our relationship since my husband sustained so many hurts from his mom.

One day when I felt afraid to go to the Lord when it seemed my performance wasn't up to par, I sensed the Lord told me: "I want to hold you, not scold you." I need to have that same attitude toward my husband.

The ABCs of Respect

As I reflected on the subject of respect, God showed me some ABCs of disrespect and then some ABCs of respect:

ABCs of disrespect: Arguing, Belittling, Condemnation
ABCs of respect: Agreeing, Building Up, Comforting

As I searched for truths about respect, I liked what one author said—that God didn't command we *feel* respect, but that we respect.

Chapter 20

Pink vs Blue

One of the situations which triggers Randy's unloving reactions to me and my withdrawal of respect, centers on this fact: God created men and women as different. It took us years to embrace that different doesn't mean wrong.

Love and Respect by Emerson Eggerichs, a book (Simon & Schuster, © 2004) and marriage retreat, helped us so much to understand differences between men and women. This author states: "The way I like to picture the difference between men and women is that the woman looks at the world through pink sunglasses that color all she sees. The man, however, looks at the world through blue sunglasses that colors all he sees. Men and women can look at precisely the same situation and see life much differently. Inevitably, their pink and blue lenses cause their interpretation of things to be at odds to some degree." (pages 32-33)

He goes on to explain: "As long as spouses do not learn to decode the pink and blue messages they are sending one another, the Crazy Cycle will spin and spin some more. What is the one thing that is going on inside of her, where the code is obviously pink? What is the one thing that is going on inside of him, where the code is obviously blue? The woman absolutely needs love, and the man absolutely needs respect…Not only is the husband commanded to love his wife, but the wife is commanded to respect her husband. You see, the husband needs respect just as much as he needs air to breathe." (pages 35 & 37)

As Randy and I remember these differences between men and women, we accept them and stop withdrawing love and respect from each other. But even if Randy fails to remember I'm different but not wrong—just female—I'm still called to show him respect.

It's not easy, but it is vital if we want to grow more in love in our marriage.

No Exceptions

But what if the man you're supposed to respect is unfaithful to you, is abusing you in any manner of ways, is addicted to something, or has emotionally checked out?

I believe God still calls us to show respect. No, we don't have to accept negative behavior, and boundaries help, but we can do it respectfully. When my husband battles sin in his life, I battle to show respect to him, especially when his sins hurt me or our whole family. But even in those times when he's hurt me emotionally, God calls me to show respect. How do I do that when I ache so much inside?

Somewhere along the line, I realized God says, "Wives, respect your husbands." This statement comes with no conditions. God doesn't say, "Wives, respect your husband when they love you the way you want to be loved." He says, "Wives, respect your husbands."

I tend to talk and talk and talk some more when my husband slips back into temper and temptresses in an attempt to convince him of the sinfulness of these behaviors and his need to repent. This method never works. And when I resort to it, respect for my husband flees. My words communicate, "You're not living your life in the right way; I'm going to tell you how to live it, and I'm going to tell you over and over and over again until you do it."

I think, *What if my husband talked on and on about my faults and failings like I do with his.* I battle different sins than my husband, but that doesn't allow me to go on and on about my plan for his deliverance from his sin areas. Yes, his sins affect me, but mine also affect him.

One day I read in Proverbs 21:19: "Better to live in a desert than with a quarrelsome and nagging wife." That described me. So I got alone in front of the mirror and practiced the utterance of two words, "You're right." While they felt difficult to say, they made a huge difference in the way Randy related to me. Saying "you're right" proved a huge step toward completion of my goal "to show respect."

Chapter 21

More Aspects of Respect

I find it hard to respect my husband when I feel unsafe in the relationship. My father yelled incessantly and said words he didn't mean in anger. I married someone who tended to do the same. As a child I felt unsafe when my father raged during one of his tirades. I've experienced that same unsafe feeling in our marriage.

The disrespect came when, instead of turning to God to feel safe, I worked hard to try to change my husband, so I could feel safe. I withdrew respect and assumed an attitude of: until I can feel safe around you, I cannot show you respect. Other behaviors which caused me to feel unsafe were when he spewed criticisms, when he rejected my opinions and emotions, when he spoke down to me, and when he lied to and deceived me. As I look over that list, I see I do those same things to Randy at times.

When I fully embrace Proverbs 18:10, I become convinced a sense of safety comes not in my marriage, but in the Lord. "The name of the Lord is a fortified tower; the righteous run to it and are safe." Yes, I communicate to my husband I don't feel safe and why, but when I demand he change a behavior he struggles with to assure my safety, I show disrespect.

I admit my husband sometimes feels unsafe with me—especially when I attempt to control him, which he says falls under the number one way I disrespect him.

False Responsibility

I realized one of the reasons I tried so hard to control instead of respect my husband was connected to my false sense of responsibility. As the oldest girl of eight children, my parents made me responsible for the wrong behaviors of my younger siblings. Because I tended to see Randy like a younger sibling (younger in the Lord), I felt responsible to get him to do the right thing, to avoid punishment from God like my parents punished me for my siblings' bad choices.

God calls me to live a holy life before my husband, but when I busy myself in attempts to change him, it manifests in a way that rejects, not respects. God will hold me accountable for my ungodly responses to his ungodly behavior—my tendency to be disrespectful.

As I respect Randy, I show acceptance of him—flaws and all. I can pray often and say occasionally how his sinful behaviors affect me and our marriage. I speak the truth gently in love instead of with demands and disdain, which are the opposite of respect.

Let Go Of Evil for Evil

Another way I show disrespect comes when I return evil for evil. Often a natural response, the Lord instead wants me to show the supernatural response to rejections in marriage.

If I claim to be the mature Christian, I need to respond with, "I refuse to hurt you back even though you hurt me." The Word says it this way, "Do not repay anyone evil for evil. Be careful to do what is right in the eyes of everyone. If it is possible, as far as it depends on you, live at peace with everyone. Do not take revenge, my dear friends, but leave room for God's wrath, for it is written: 'It is mine to avenge; I will repay,' says the Lord... Do not be overcome by evil, but overcome evil with good" (Romans 12:17-19,21).

An illustration of this happened years ago when I locked myself out of our apartment. I called Randy at work to come home and let me in.

"Only stupid people lock themselves out of their own houses," he shouted angrily.

That time I chose not to yell back at him for his insults. In a matter of days he locked his keys in his car and had to call me to open the car for him. He humbly apologized.

I realized I can't maintain an attitude of revenge and an attitude of respect at the same time. Revenge—the pursuit of getting even—a trap set by the enemy, keeps me from forward progress after hurt and heartache. It endangers my marriage, and robs me of peace, and puts a distance not only between me and my husband, but also between me and the Lord.

Respect and Decision-Making

One of the areas where I show disrespect comes when my husband makes decisions—especially when I don't agree with the decision he makes.

Years ago at an in-home art show, the person who led the party taught a phrase which stuck with me. If one person loved a piece of art and another person said "Yuck," she could lose the sale. Also, "yuck" showed unkindness and lack of respect for differences in taste.

Randy and I took that statement into our marriage, and I realize when I "yuck" Randy's "wow," I show disrespect. He reminds me of this when he says, "You just yucked my wow." This can be in simple matters, like what restaurant to dine at and home decoration issues as well as larger issues like where to move and how to invest our money, but it still comes across as disrespect when I do it. I pray for God to give me grace to do what that artwork presenter said, "Don't yuck his wow."

God's Command To Respect

There is no doubt that the Lord wants me to show respect to my husband. In the Amplified version of the Bible He spells it out this way: "and the wife [must see to it] that she respects and delights in her husband [that she notices him and prefers him and treats him with loving concern, treasuring him, honoring him, and holding him dear]" (Ephesians 5:33). As I determine to respect my husband—no matter how he treats me and even in his most unloving moments—amazing changes happen in my heart and in our marriage.

Lord, thank You for teaching me how much my husband needs respect. Please reveal to me more ways to show respect. Heal my hurts and my desire for revenge which get in the way of respecting my husband. In Jesus' name. Amen.

Part IX

Submission: A Worthy Mission

Love...is not self-seeking... —1 Corinthians 13:4-5

It is in willing submission rather than
grudging capitulation that the woman in the church
(whether married or single) and the wife in the home
find their fulfillment. —Elisabeth Elliot

Chapter 22

Learning to Submit

Ileft my husband early in our marriage—on our honeymoon, over a point of submission, though I failed to realize it at the time. We stopped in Jackson Hole, Wyoming, (part of our tour of the West) and Randy wanted to wait until after dark to eat dinner. Already 8pm (Chicago time) and with no lunch, I stated my case about being famished, but he didn't care. He wanted a late dinner.

So I walked away. *How can I live with this man who won't even let me eat when I'm hungry? Is that what marriage is all about—to give up your way of doing things and submit to an ogre who won't consider what you want?*

I walked around the town and felt sorry for myself. Marrying Randy seemed like the biggest mistake of my life but staying married to him seemed as difficult a task as climbing up one side and sliding down the other of the antler arch in the center of town. But I still didn't get anything to eat. I felt too angry for that. Without an easy way to find each other since this was before cell phones, (I could have gone back to the car but didn't think about it), miraculously after about an hour, our paths crossed. We made up, and went to dinner. Since that day,

I learned to carry snacks to deal with a husband who went up to twelve hours without eating.

My "separation" from my husband that day centered on one problem—my insistence on my own way. He insisted on his way as well. But God taught me over the years that to "submit as a wife" I state my case, and if he rejects it, I say, "OK honey, we'll do it your way."

Good Advice From the "Love Verses"

Years later, at the wedding ceremony of a friend of mine, I sat alone because Randy's schedule prevented his attendance. Once again, as at so many weddings, the pastor read the love verses from 1 Corinthians 13: "Love is patient, love is kind…"

For the first time, words from that section of Scripture seemed louder than any of the others to my soul. The pastor used a translation other than the one I usually read, and he said, "Love does not insist on its own way." At that moment I realized so much of the conflict in our marriage came because I did just that. To politely ask for, or gently suggest something I needed, failed to fit into my way of communicating what I wanted or needed from my husband. I lived too often in an "I insist on my way" mode. Another word for insist came to mind back then: demand.

That day, I asked God to change my heart. I admitted I tended to determine my way was wiser than Randy's—especially since I stayed immersed in the Word, and my husband didn't. But many times our conflicts didn't center on matters of right and wrong, but just whose way to choose.

Later, I learned the reason God commanded wives submit to their husbands. With two people involved, if they disagree, someone needs to act as the tie-breaker. God chose the husband for that. Over time, I learned to celebrate that fact.

Let Go Of Making Demands

Sometime after the wedding where God seemed to shout out one of my major issues, I read the Bible all the way through and chose to do so with a Bible called *The Every Day With Jesus Bible.* (Holman Bible Publishers 2004) Within that Bible I read devotions by Selwyn Hughes. As I read, the word "demand" once again confronted me, and conviction cornered me. He wrote: "This sin is probably more deeply buried in our hearts than any other.... The sin I refer to is—demandingness. You won't find the word in the Bible, but you *will* certainly see it illustrated there. Demandingness is insisting that our interests be served irrespective of others. Clearly, if Christ is to live in us, this has to die in us." (page 42)

He goes on to say: "We demand that people treat us in the way we believe they should. We demand that people support us in times of trouble. We demand that no one comes close to hurting us in the way that we might have been hurt in childhood. Wedged tightly in the recesses of our heart is this ugly splinter that, if not removed, will produce a poison that will infect every part of our lives." (page 58)

I saw clearly I battled a demanding attitude in my life and in our marriage.

One Aspect of Demandingness

Another word connected to the word "demand," which shows a lack of submission is control. One counselor said to approach my husband with curiosity rather than the desire to control. Curiosity centers on the desire to know him better rather than an attitude of "I know you better than you know yourself, so I need to show you through demands how to change." And when it came to decisions or announcements of what I wanted him to do, the counselor suggested I invite rather than demand.

The bottom line came to this: If I demand of my husband, I fail to be in the position of submission.

Chapter 23

The Battle To Submit

Submission does not come naturally for women. In fact, I and many other women I know, tend toward seeking to gain control in marriage rather than submitting to our husbands.

Depending On God

So if God knows we women desire control, and He knows it presents such difficulty for us to submit, why does He give us the command in the New Testament to submit to our husbands? "Wives, submit yourselves unto your own husbands..." (Galatians 5:22 KJV). The answer is that I can't do it unless I depend on Him. The more I see I fail at it, the greater my desire to seek Him, and the more like Him I'll become. Jesus submitted to the Father, and God wants to gently mold me more to Jesus' image.

Often when I hurt, I forget completely about submission. When my husband wounds me, I think my vows to honor, cherish, and submit to him no longer apply. At times I mistakenly think marriage should never hurt, instead of recognizing it correctly as a blend of joy and sorrow which teaches me (if I let it) to love like Jesus. Suffering in marriage serves a purpose—to make me more like Christ. I need to submit to the transformation process in order to come forth as gold. (See Job 23:10)

Submission to God

I find I cannot submit to my husband unless I first submit to God. The second half of Galatians 5:22 does say "...as unto the Lord" (KJV) Often I believe I can't submit to Randy because he hasn't completely submitted to God. At times he seems so far from the Lord, and yet God calls me to submit so long as what he calls me to submit to do is not a sin against God.

The Bible—God's Word of life—helps me to submit as I submerge myself in it. I know the Bible works when I apply it to the death processes that threaten our marriage at times. I discovered if I feel "I'm dying inside," or "this marriage is dying," it's often because I need to work more on dying to myself and stop my attempts to control.

Unlike our culture and the worldly Christian culture, the Word doesn't encourage me to ditch my spouse or change to a different spouse, but instructs me to let God change me from a rebellious, "I-must-have-my-own-way" spouse to one who embraces love, forgiveness, mercy, and that dirty S-word—submission.

Chapter 24

Benefits of Submission

As I stop looking at submission as a dirty word, I discover good comes out of obedience in this area.

Safety in Submission

Sometimes I worry if I submit to my husband, and he makes the wrong decision, the blame will fall to me. Not true. In the work place, if I give an excellent idea to my boss and she rejects it, the CEO does not blame me. My boss must suffer the greatest consequences. Yes, her wrong decision may affect my life, but the consequences fall on the boss and not on me. This proves true in marriage as well. When I try to force my husband to make a decision which seems right to me, I create discord. The proper One to "force" him to make the right decision is the Lord.

Such a scenario happened in our marriage several years ago. Randy wanted to move to the Reno, Nevada area, and as I prayed about this, I received no affirmation from the Lord. Our granddaughter urgently needed us because our daughter lived as a single mom. Also, my mother and dad lived three hours from us in Florida, and my dad suffered from a disability, so

I went there often to help out and give encouragement. How difficult and expensive to fly thousands of miles back to Florida when they needed me. My mind came up with other arguments against the move, which I voiced to my husband. After I stated my case with no demands, I decided to submit to what he wanted to do, and leave it in the Lord's hands.

Then we went for a visit to the area where my husband said we would pick out a neighborhood in which to live. As we looked at homes, I still didn't feel any release or desire in my soul to move there, but I kept silent. After being in Reno several days, my husband woke me up early in the morning.

"I have to talk to you," he said with urgency.

"What happened?" I asked.

"God said we are not to move here—at least not now," and he continued with, "He woke me in the middle of the night to tell me that."

My husband rarely voices, "The Lord told me…," but how I rejoiced that God spoke and Randy listened. I learned that day if I would stop my attempts to be God to Randy, He would do His part and speak to my husband in crucial areas. Other times, Randy made a wrong decision, which taught him to depend more on my insights, but especially on the need to seek the Lord for counsel.

Another Lesson in Submission

Another time, I felt led to hand my husband the telephone when a troubled relative from his side of the family called in search of a place to live. He lived with us for a time in the past with disastrous results. In the phone conversation, he tried to convince me he and drugs parted ways, and how he felt serious about his pursuit of God and wanted to make a permanent change in his life. I gave the phone to Randy, which seemed to go against my better judgment.

Randy invited him to come live with us. As time passed, we discovered this relative still battled drug addiction and refused our efforts to help him find a drug rehab program. He conned my husband for a time, who seemed blind to his manipulation. This caused us both to depend more fully on the Lord. At times I told myself, *What a mistake; why did I hand Randy the phone? Why didn't I just say "no?"* But God did a work in Randy's life through this difficult time with someone who pretended to seek God and proved to be a liar, a thief, and possibly a sociopath. That time actually brought us closer together as I submitted to Randy when everything in me shouted, "Get this person out of our home."

Finally Randy said, "You need to leave."

But it happened in the Lord's time table, not mine.

How often my heart proclaimed *This is not my plan; this isn't how things should be.* I learned I need to let go of my plan, which makes submission to Randy easier.

Chapter 25

More Challenges In Regard To Submission

It can feel difficult to submit to my husband when it seems he isn't submitting to the Lord. Yet as I seek the Lord to guide me as to how to submit, He's faithful to do just that.

Submission To His Spiritual Leadership

I confess I try to take charge when Randy reneges on his rightful position as the spiritual leader of our home. Several years ago, I thought of how at Thanksgiving dinner, Randy often instructed me to say the prayer even though I longed for him to do it. Also, I wanted badly for us to go around the table and offer thanks for a special blessing that year. A part of me on this particular Thanksgiving wanted to take control and urge him to say the prayer and to have us go around the table. In other words, I wanted to dictate how he should lead.

Instead I gave the matter to the Lord and said, "Even if there's no prayer and no voicing our thanks, I'll accept that. I won't try to make it happen. Also, if Randy asks me to say the prayer, I will, and won't demand he do it."

On that Thanksgiving, Randy said a prayer that brought all of us to tears as we remembered my brother who died by suicide months before. He also voiced we needed to go around the table and give thanks for a blessing or two—the first time he'd done that. As I got out of the way and stopped my attempts to control and determined to submit, my husband led.

Submission Leads to Peace

A number of years ago, I got so worked up over Randy's sliding back into looking at porn, I ended up in the hospital. My blood pressure went up, and the doctor thought I had suffered a TIA.

The problem came when I refused to submit to the Lord or to Randy.

When I discovered Randy's backsliding, the Lord gave me two instructions: "Keep your focus on me," and "Be silent." Randy asked that we not talk about it because it upset me so much, but I did the opposite. I obsessively kept my focus on the problem of porn in our marriage, and I refused to stay silent about the issue. The more I talked, the more defensive and less repentant Randy became, and the more devastated I felt. I realized later, if I submitted to the Lord, and to Randy, when he asked we not talk about the issue, peace would have reigned.

One day, months after I discovered Randy's relapse, I found these words written on a piece of paper by his computer: "RE-SPECT—Your Savior—Your Wife—Women—yourself."

Too often in marriage I think if I gain control in my marriage, I'll find peace. But Isaiah 26:3 holds the key to peace: "Thou wilt keep him in perfect peace, whose mind is stayed on thee..." (KJV).

Let Love Control

The Lord needs repeatedly to chasten me with, "I am in control." Recently, when I tried to look up the song, "God is in Control," by Twila Paris, I inadvertently typed, "Love is in control." If I leave matters to God and let go of my attempts to control the situation, love remains in control. As I submit to God, rather than insisting on my own way, His love flows through me. My attempts to control my husband come from fear, and fear never produces a good outcome in our marriage. I need to remember submission demonstrates love for my husband. And joy flows from true submission.

Lord, help me to submit first of all to You and then to my husband. Let me see submission as a positive and not a negative. Continue to show me what it means to be a submissive wife and let me do it with a godly attitude. In Jesus' name I pray. Amen.

Part X

The Gift of a Gentle Wife

Love…is not easily angered. —1 Corinthians 13:4-5

Anger devours almost all other good emotions.
It deadens the soul. It numbs the heart to joy
and gratitude and hope and tenderness and
compassion and kindness. —John Piper

Chapter 26

Stop Focusing on His Anger

For years I focused only on Randy's anger and how it hurt me.

"I can't take this anymore!" I wailed on some days. My husband's angry outbursts—like land mines—seemed hard to avoid. No physical violence occurred, but often I felt blown apart emotionally by his shouting, profanity, and belligerence. Some days I wondered, *Is my only choice to leave this marriage before his anger destroys me?*

Along the way God gave me tools to deal with my husband's anger—from His Word, from counselors, and from excellent books like *Angry Men and The Women Who Love Them* by Paul Hegstrom, Ph.D.

I saw my husband in what Hegstrom wrote: "In our communications we hear through our filters—our perceptions of what someone is trying to tell us… When the filtering system is filled with traumatic wounds that clog our perceptions, it keeps us from seeing reality.

"One who is wounded in this way tries to love, tries to resolve conflict, and manage his or her anger as normal healthy adults do… but can't see reality or truth and can't resolve his conflicts because it can't get through the filtering system… He or she doesn't see reality—only the perception of everything that happens and things said in conversation... Because these perceptions aren't dealt with and conflicts aren't resolved, the person gets frustrated and lives in a rage." (Kindle DX, 26%/ 571-581/Chapter 3)

God helped my husband deal with his traumas, but effects still plague him. These days I spend less time and effort in attempts to get Randy to deal with his anger. Instead God urges me to focus on my own anger and become a gentle, rather than an angry, wife. I see at times I, too, have trouble with my perception of reality because of my traumas.

Admitting To My Own Anger Issues

"You always remain calm; you never get mad," a friend said to me years ago.

I battled anger, but often denied its presence. I pretended only my husband possessed an anger problem. Once I opened my eyes, I realized my anger presented itself differently than his. Mine tended to be the slow, seething kind, which I convinced myself proved superior because it was quieter—except for the times I finally exploded from no more room to push my anger down.

"You're a gunny sacker," Randy accused.

When I admitted the accuracy of his statement—that I tended to push down my anger and hold on to it—I realized I also got back at Randy with passive-aggressive means, like when I withdrew from him or spent too much money. Sometimes I brought up the details of my anger weeks or months after the original offense.

Along the way I realized I made this vow: I refuse to exhibit anger. I saw how my father lost control often, and I didn't want to do that. I feared I would hurt people the way he hurt me. I renounced the vow and asked God how to deal with my anger His way, so I wouldn't deny anger and stuff it down with explosions on a regular basis.

Often I felt depressed because I turned my anger inward. I could hold only so much inside, so intermittently I exploded (mostly at home)—especially when I battled PMS. I remember early in our marriage, I threw a pan of spaghetti sauce across the room because Randy criticized how it tasted. Other times I broke dishes. Denial, depression, explosion became the cycle I went through repeatedly when it came to my issues with anger. Even though I wanted to believe Randy's anger presented the major problem in our marriage because he expressed his anger more loudly, lewdly, and frequently, I realized mine proved just as destructive.

Chapter 27

Dealing with My Anger

To deal with my anger in a better way I discovered these steps:

Admit You Feel Angry

Anger isn't sinful, but what I do with my anger can lead to a sinful act. When I denied anger, I disobeyed God, who says in Scripture to be angry but not sin. (See Ephesians 4:26.) The irony of my denial hit me when I insisted I did it to avoid a negative response, but in the end, my response became more negative than if I admitted—and dealt with—my anger promptly.

Sometimes, I denied I felt angry because I became deluded and believed good wives don't get angry. Once I allowed myself to admit anger, I worked hard to take care not to answer Randy's anger with the same kind he dished out and with the same volume and, at times, vulgarity.

Stop and Think

Once I admitted anger, the goal became to avoid a destructive response. As a Christian I learned the Holy Spirit resides in the gap between, "I feel angry," and my response to it.

To avoid sin when angry, I find it helpful to take time to think, through removal from the scene, when I feel anger rise. Following this Scripture helps tremendously: "Tremble [with anger or fear], and do not sin; Meditate in your heart upon your bed and be still [reflect on your sin and repent of your rebellion]. Selah" (Psalm 4:4 AMP).

When I first started this, my husband asked, "Where did you disappear to?"

"I had to think," I explained.

Once I thought about why I became angry, or finished my journal entry about my anger, and prayers for God to intervene, my tendency to impulsively and angrily lash out diminished, and I could communicate clearly regarding the conflict.

Assess Expectations and Demands

Over time I realized the root of my anger centered on unrealistic expectations. Often these expectations turned into demands.

One demand which ruled me centered on: "I demand you change and be the way I think you should be." So when I ask myself, "Why am I so angry?" I can also ask, "What demands come with my anger?"

For example, when my husband forgets or fails to accomplish a task he said he would, when anger rises over this, I ask, "Lord, will You show me my demands?" It may be, "I demand he never forget or fail to do what I want him to do." When I assess demands, I look for key words like "never" and "always."

I discovered I need to give my rigid expectations and demands to the Lord and ask Him to heal areas of my life from which they originate.

Talk About Anger

Rather than "you" statements ("You make me so mad"), I learned to use "I" statements, which prove to less likely bring on defensiveness and anger in my husband. Beyond that, I also learned not to say merely, "I feel *so mad* at you." Instead I use these underlying words a counselor suggested to express anger: "I feel *frustrated* when …," "I feel *afraid* when …," "I feel *hurt* when …." since beneath anger can be frustration, fear, or hurt.

I learned to avoid a harsh tone to talk through my anger, a practice I developed when my husband used a harsh tone with me. The advice in Proverbs 15:1 really works: "A gentle answer turns away wrath, but a harsh word stirs up anger." A gentle answer turns away not only my husband's wrath, but also my own.

Sometimes the Lord leads me to talk only to Him about my anger toward Randy because He knows at that point Randy refuses to hear me. How cleansing to pour out my anger to the Lord. Sometimes I take a walk to do this, or write in my journal. No matter what I say to the Lord, He can take it. He won't lash back as a person might—even if my anger becomes directed at Him, i.e., for His seeming lack of intervention in Randy's life.

Let Go of Anger

When I hold on to anger, a sinful response becomes more likely. Once I ask myself, "Why am I so angry?" and take steps to communicate anger, I need to let go of it. Ephesians 4:26-27 states, "…Do not let the sun go down while you are still angry, and do not give the devil a foothold."

A thought process I determine to avoid is this: "I will let go of my anger when he lets go of his, or pours kindness on me, or apologizes." I also assess if my anger originates with sins such as unforgiveness, hatred, or self-centeredness and confess those. Then I ask God to empower me to offer a godly response.

With some hurtful situations, my anger glows anew in the morning, even though I let go of it the night before. Sometimes I need to let go repeatedly, especially as the enemy tempts me to be angry again. He whispers, "Don't forget how much he hurt you." Then I find I relive the painful incident and re-feel it. The word resent means to "re-feel." The enemy wants me to carry resentment daily, but I can say, "No."

Some might say to let go of anger proves to be a weakness. I discovered when I allow the Lord to help me with my anger issues, I count on His strength. I can become a gentler wife when I learn to control my anger, instead of allowing it to control me. To "be angry and sin not" becomes a reality, but only when I invite God to involve Himself in the process. As I commit my emotions to Him, He shows me a way—His way—to handle anger in my life.

Learn to Listen

Part of the process to become a gentle, instead of an angry wife, centers on a willingness to listen.

Both Randy and I tend to get angry when ignored. I often fail to get him to listen to me, but I can choose to listen to him rather than focus on my insistence he hear me. As I adopt a gentle attitude and demeanor, I find it easier to listen. Anger tends to make me deaf to what my spouse says.

Chapter 28

Gentle and Strong

Ican be gentle as I grow in strength—not in human strength but in the strength of the Lord. In Nehemiah 8:10 I read: "... Do not grieve, for the joy of the Lord is your strength." Another verse about strength is Philippians 4:13 "I can do all things [which He has called me to do] through Him who strengthens and empowers me..." (AMP).

In my marriage I spent much time and effort in attempts to look beautiful, but in 1 Peter 3:2-4 God reminds me: "Your beauty...should be that of your inner self, the unfading beauty of a gentle and quiet spirit, which is of great worth in God's sight."

I remember when I read those words for the first time and many times after, I said,

"That sounds impossible." I realized I battled the opposite— anger and contentiousness.

Now I pray, "Lord, I long to be more and more a quiet and gentle wife. Let me grow in that with your help and strength."

Put My Dukes Down

Years ago, I read a book which told how, if we possess residual anger from our childhoods, we tend to walk around with our dukes up. Some people call it defensiveness. Randy and I both battle this problem. Since we each had anger issues in connection to our opposite sex parent, for years if I did anything which reminded Randy of his mother, he tended to respond with anger and sometimes rage. If Randy did anything which reminded me of my dad, it brought on emotional upheaval and often anger. I remember Randy shouted in years past, "I am not your father." I worked through much of the anger issues in regard to my dad. At this point—even though Randy's mom died a number of years ago—he still battles deep-seated anger and unforgiveness toward her. I have to choose to refuse to take it personally when he overreacts in anger because of some trigger which inadvertently sets him off—sometimes through an innocent comment or gesture I make.

I told Randy in a counseling session I considered this: "I will put an enlarged photo of your mother in front of my face to remind you and me that your anger, although directed toward me, really centers on your mother."

"That would only upset me more," he said, "I don't want to see her face."

With that comment, he realized the truth of what I said.

Even if Randy refuses to exhibit gentleness, I certainly can. I came a long way, or rather I should say, God brought me a long way from my dish-breaking, spaghetti-sauce-throwing days. And Randy makes progress as well when it comes to his anger issues.

Chapter 29

More About Anger and Gentleness

In a session with a counselor a while ago, he talked to me about passivity. I realized when Randy flew into a rage, I frequently chose a passive reaction. I said and did nothing. For years I viewed this as forgiveness and acceptance. But my heart felt the opposite. I laid up anger and bitterness inside. Also, the counselor brought up that it taught my husband how to treat me.

As I reflected on passivity, I realized at times I lashed out in anger at Randy when I let go of my passive response. God taught me somewhere between aggressive anger and total passivity lies the place He wants me to occupy. From that place, I speak the truth in love and express my feelings, but not in a hostile way.

One day Randy raged at me for a variety of minor issues. In the midst of his tirade, God gave me this sentence to say, and I said it in the most gentle way possible: "This anger you expressed just now has little to do with me. It centers on your insecurity as a man."

Suddenly Randy quieted. That truth, spoken in a gentle way, hit home.

Actions Instead of Words

On other occasions, as I become aware words won't work to stop Randy's angry outbursts, I discover communication with actions does. When he rages, I leave the room rather than "taking it" like I did as a child with my father, and at other times in our marriage. Also, I even leave our home for a while, i.e., to go on a walk. At times, I go to visit my elderly parents who live on the other side of the state.

When Randy sometimes asks me why I need to go visit them, I tell him (but not in a way that accuses) "To encourage and help them and also to get away from your anger and find some peace." I ask God to give me the grace to say it in a gentle, nonjudgmental way. When I get home I sweetly say, "No one yelled at me the whole time, and it felt great." Praise the Lord, God completely delivered my dad from his yelling, rage-filled ways, so each time I visit, I celebrate that fact and know God will continue to deliver Randy.

Randy desires to let go of anger, but he holds to natural responses and finds it hard at times to allow God to intervene, so he can become free from what some call a hair-trigger temper.

Fear Can Be At the Root of Anger

God reminds me, at the root of Randy's anger lies fear. Instead of anger in return, I can speak to his fear instead of to his anger. "Honey, don't panic. It's going to be OK."

I then remind him of God's promises and of God's faithfulness to us as a couple.

One wife, who's been married for over 40 years, told me: "I knew I had to stand my ground (against her husband's wrong behavior) but I was doing it in the wrong way—with hatred, anger, and revenge." God pointed her to Philippians 4:8 in order to make her into a gentler wife: "…whatever is true, whatever is noble, whatever is right, whatever is admirable—if anything is excellent or praiseworthy—think about such things." When I respond to my husband with anger rather than gentleness, I need to confess to my husband and to God—even if my anger seems triggered by his.

Learn to Hear Despite the Anger

The Lord instructed me to listen to Randy and hear beyond his tone. Many times, what he says presents truth, but the way he says it makes me want to reject every word. One day, he overheard my talk with my daughter about someone who wronged our family by the theft of $4000 through check fraud when we tried to help him. My husband decided not to press criminal charges. That day I felt especially angry toward this unsaved man who took advantage of the kindness of Christians. Randy shouted at me harshly and threw in a few curse words to tell me how he hated the fact I gave in to a judgmental and vengeful attitude. Instead of a gentle response, I yelled back and defended my position and declared him wrong.

I resisted his words of truth because of how he said them. Later, I admitted the truth of what he said, repented of my wrong attitude toward him, and chose forgiveness as I returned to my prayers for this person's salvation.

My Desire to Be a Gentle Wife

If I want to be a gentle wife, I need to open my heart to learn from Jesus who says in Scripture: "…learn from me, for I am gentle and lowly in heart…" (Matthew 11:29).

One day, while I walked up the stairs at church, I battled anger toward my husband. A part of me felt proud I kept my mouth shut and abstained from my temptation to blast him for his latest verbal assault. On the floor, I found a small card with these few words from Scripture on it: "...in quietness and trust is your strength" (Isaiah 30:15). Even though I refrained from an angry eruption, the reason anger continued to churn inside became clear. I failed to trust the Lord or entrust the problem to Him.

When Randy becomes trapped by sin, whether it be anger or pornography, Galatians 6:1 reminds me not to use anger or self-righteousness to confront him. Instead God gives this instruction: "...if someone is caught in a sin, you who live by the Spirit should restore that person gently..."

New Reactions to Anger

I praise God for changes He brought about in my reactions to Randy's anger and also in the resolution of anger issues in my own life. God draws me closer to the role of a quiet and gentle wife, and it helps our relationship so much. When I think of gentleness toward Randy—no matter what he does against me—I think of the gentleness of the Lord. When I go to Him, and my soul feels tossed in turmoil, or I feel anger boil up to the surface, I'm amazed by how He gently holds me, whispers truth to my soul, and calms me with His love.

Even when his anger erupts, I can gently calm my husband with the Lord's love which flows through me—once I go to Him and allow Him to quiet me with His love. God's love which flows through me, does calm my husband. Gentle love does that to a person.

Lord, I praise You that it's possible for me to be a gentle wife. Help me to grow in that as I let go of anger toward my husband, even if he won't let go of anger toward me. In Jesus' name I pray. Amen.

121

Part XI

Remove Roadblocks to Forgiveness

Love… does not take into account a wrong endured.
—1 Corinthians 13:4-5 AMP

We are most like beasts when we kill;
we are most like men when we judge; we are most like
God when we forgive. —Source unknown

Chapter 30

Letting Go of Myths About Forgiveness

"Even as the angry, vengeful thoughts boiled through me, I saw the sin of them. Jesus Christ himself had died for this man; was I going to ask for more? *Lord Jesus, I prayed, forgive me and help me to forgive him.*

"I tried to smile. I struggled to raise my hand. I could not. I felt nothing, not the slightest spark of warmth or charity. And so again I breathed a silent prayer.

"Jesus. I cannot forgive him. Give me your forgiveness.

"As I took his hand, mechanically, woodenly, a most incredible thing happened. From my shoulder along my arm and through my hand a current seemed to pass from me to him, while into my heart sprang a love for this stranger that almost overwhelmed me.

"And so I discovered that it is not on our forgiveness any more than on our goodness that the world's healing hinges, but on His. When He tells us to love our enemies, He gives along with the command, the love itself." (Corrie ten Boom, *Tramp for the Lord*, Revell 1974, pages 53-55.)

I first read about Corrie ten Boom's struggle to forgive one of the Nazi guards who came to hear her speak after the war even as I fought to forgive my husband in the midst of an especially difficult time in our marriage.

I knew it was wrong to refuse to forgive. As I prayed, God revealed seven myths I believed which prevented the flow of forgiveness through me to my husband. As I let go of these, I moved on into the forgiveness process:

Myth #1: I must wait for my husband to say, "I'm sorry."

I wasted a lot of time in repeated recalls of the wrongs Randy did, in my attempts to coerce an apology from him. As God dealt with me, I determined to forgive without "ifs" attached—"If he says 'I'm sorry,' and if I decide he really is, then I'll forgive." Jesus forgave while He hung on the cross. (See Luke 23:34) None of the soldiers that put him to death said, "I'm really sorry for what we did to you." Yet He said, "Father, forgive them…"

Myth #2: I must feel like forgiving.

Forgiveness is a choice of the will. Sometimes positive emotions follow the choice to forgive Randy. Other times, I battle hurts for quite a while. Along the way, I've learned that no matter how I feel, if I determine to maintain an attitude of forgiveness, I win in the end. When I reach out and bless my husband even when I don't feel like it, I succeed.

Myth #3 Certain actions should never be forgiven.

No sins Randy commits against me are too big to forgive, since God has called me to "…Forgive as the Lord forgave you," (Colossians 3:13) and He is One "who forgives all your sins…" (Psalm 103:3) At times, I try to convince myself exceptions exist when it comes to forgiveness. If I choose to hold back forgiveness for these "exceptions," I've been the one to suffer. As a mental health worker, I see more suffering because a person refuses to forgive an abuser than because of the abuse. A quote

I heard awhile back speaks of this: "Bitterness is the poison you drink thinking it will kill another person."

Myth #4 To say "I forgive" means, "What he did isn't wrong."
To utter "I forgive you," doesn't release Randy from the truth that he did wrong. It means God released me from the pursuit of vengeance for what he did. True forgiveness means I leave the justice to the Father as Jesus did. "When they hurled their insults at him, he did not retaliate; when he suffered he made no threats. Instead, he entrusted himself to him who judges justly" (1 Peter 2:23).

Myth #5 Unforgiveness will force my husband to change.
I learned my anger does not serve to motivate my husband to stop hurting me. God uses a different tactic to get us to turn from our sins. In fact, the Bible says "God's kindness is intended to lead you toward repentance." (Romans 2:4) What gets people to change, and have sorrowful hearts in regard to sin comes as a result of kindness —even when they don't deserve it. Joseph did this with his brothers who sold him into slavery. (See Genesis 50:15-21) His kindness and mercy made a life-changing impact on them.

Myth # 6: Unforgiveness protects me from further hurt.
In former days, I developed the habit of erecting a wall of bitterness to keep from further hurt. Unfortunately, this wall also kept me from closeness to Randy and to the Lord. As I let God protect me, He remains faithful to do so. "He will cover you with his feathers, and under his wings you will find refuge..." (Psalm 91:4).

Myth #7: Unforgiveness Makes Me Stronger
Some people called me "a strong woman." Yet I learned, instead of a truly strong heart, I maintained a hardened heart.

Years of refusal to forgive hardened it, so I lost my sense of compassion and tenderness. I want to be strong as the Lord defines it—someone able to resist temptation, especially the temptation to hold on to unforgiveness. Once I let it go, I notice real strength displayed in my life.

Sometimes these myths—these lies from the enemy—come back and wrap themselves around my heart. Through prayer and asking God for a softened heart, I arrive back at the place of forgiveness. Meditation on the mercy of Christ helps me keep bitterness out of my heart in my marriage.

Chapter 31

The Necessity of Forgiveness

I like what Grace Fox writes in her book *10-Minute Time Outs for Busy Women:* "When we think about what Jesus Christ did for us, how can we even consider withholding forgiveness from one who offends us? Extending forgiveness is not easy, but it's not optional in God's eyes. Withholding forgiveness places chains around our heart. It breeds bitterness. It builds a wall between us and the offender—and worse, between us and God. But following His example sets us free. It breaks the chains, banishes bitterness, razes the wall, and rebuilds broken relationships." (Harvest House 2005, page 126)

One of the bad habits I developed when it came to my refusal to forgive, centered on my search for people who agreed with my bitterness. I remember phone calls to people to tell them about the latest offenses of my husband. I chose carefully in this matter. Obviously, other bitter people serve as the best people to figuratively "sign my petition" to hold on to unforgiveness.

God sees it as wrong when I seek others to encourage me to hold onto my unforgiveness and bitterness. I not only hurt others, but myself as well. This verse convinces me of that truth: "See to it that no one falls short of the grace of God and that no bitter root grows up to cause trouble and defile many" (Hebrews 12:15).

How ironic that, in my attitude of unforgiveness, I often preached to others about forgiving—especially my children.

The True Root of Misery

Often I claimed to be miserable because of my husband's evil deeds. But the parable in Matthew 18:23-35 showed me my misery truly comes because I refuse to forgive. A man, forgiven a huge debt, then refused to forgive someone a much smaller debt. The consequence came: "And in wrath his master turned him over to the torturers (jailers) until he paid all that he owed" (verse 34). In the next verse, the Lord confronts me with this: "My heavenly Father will also do the same to [every one of] you, if each of you does not forgive his brother from your heart" (AMP). How often I resided in that place of torture in my married life because I withheld forgiveness. Once I let go, I felt as if a prison door opened.

An incident comes to mind, which happened a number of years ago. One day deep into our marriage, I caught Randy with porn—again. He stayed away for years, but during an especially stressful time, which extended over many months, he slipped when he opened x-rated emails repeatedly. The especially hurtful blow came because his backsliding happened at the time we renewed our wedding vows. I specifically told him I wanted to do it because of the line, "forsaking all others." Instead of choosing honesty about his continued struggle, and/or a refusal to renew our vows, or a postponement, he deceived me.

I felt devastated—not because of his relapse—but because of the deception. *Certainly I can't forgive him for this,* my emotions screamed, and I considered a separation. Bitterness convinced me my past forgiveness kept him locked in to the problem. *Now*

I will hold my ground and not forgive until he changes, I promised myself. My thoughts of separation became part of my revenge as I reflected on a way to try to humiliate him into change.

For over a week, my anger boiled. I cried bitter tears. I yelled. I blamed. I shamed. I tried to get him to understand how I felt. I wailed self-pity prayers. All of this soaked in bitterness.

I failed to go to God's Word for guidance. Why should I? God hadn't changed my husband. Now I would do it—my way—through anger and unforgiveness. When I finally opened my Bible, one of the first verses I read jumped off the page: "...human anger does not produce the righteousness that God desires" (James 1:20).

As soon as I let go of anger and chose forgiveness, my torment subsided, and peace prevailed. I felt more love than ever toward my husband, and my heart overflowed with compassion for how he suffered because of his bondage. I knew deep down he wanted to let go, but felt unable to. Once I forgave him, everything no longer centered on me.

Chapter 32

Willing To Forgive

When forgiveness seems impossible, an incident from years ago, when our youngest daughter was a preschooler, comes to mind:

In the morning, I stood at the kitchen sink and washed dishes, overwhelmed by that familiar this-time-I-just-cannot-forgive-him feeling. The words he hurled at me the evening before still stung. I felt unable to focus on my possible contribution to the fight, because my hurt consumed me. Although I wanted to obey God and forgive, I allowed the sun to go down on my anger. The best I could muster came through as a scribbled line in my journal before I went to bed, "Lord, make me willing to forgive."

Randy avoided the kitchen and headed for the door, while Melissa, then age three, shouted, "Daddy, let's play."

"I've got to go to work, Honey," Randy said.

"My kiss! My kiss!" Melissa bellowed and raced after him to give her good-bye kiss.

Anytime Randy or I went anywhere, she insisted on a kiss and a hug.

"A hug! A hug!" I could imagine her stretching her arms up and jumping up and down.

Hurry, I thought, as I waited expectantly for the door to close.

"What about Mommy?" Melissa asked.

Why can't children mind their own business? I hoped Randy would ignore her.

"You didn't give her a kiss and a hug."

Melissa never took notice of how we said good-bye to each other before, at least to my recollection. Why today?

"I don't think she wants one," answered Randy.

Well, he's right about that. Now please leave. But Melissa couldn't let it rest. She raced into the kitchen with a shocked look on her face.

"Mommy, do you want a kiss and a hug?"

Her eyes, wide and filled with innocence, looked up at me. I know she saw me not as a bundle of anger, but as a dispenser of love. My heart felt torn. I felt unready to let go of my hurt, but neither did I want to cause her pain. How could I lie and say "yes," when a kiss was the last thing I wanted?

In that moment between her question and my answer, it seemed God asked, "Are you willing?" He presented me with the opportunity to take the first step toward restoration of peace in my relationship with Randy.

I felt forced into this. What a choice! If I disobeyed God and refused to forgive, I would hurt my daughter. God backed me into a corner. Yet, wasn't that what I prayed for—"Lord, *make me* willing?"

"Yes," I said to my daughter's question and to God's question, "Are you willing?"

Melissa ran out to get her dad, jubilant she proved him wrong. The joyful reconciler dragged him by the hand to the kitchen.

"Now give Mommy a kiss," she instructed sweetly and gave a triumphant smile when he did so.

"Now a hug," she urged. We hugged, and with that hug the wall of hurt within me began to melt. Forgiveness no longer seemed an impossibility.

Soon after it happened, I wrote down the above recollection of that day, and I read it often. When I invite God into the conflicts and crises of my married life, He gives me grace to forgive, even when my emotions tell me it's impossible.

Someone once told me God does not give me any commands in the Bible without supplying the grace to carry out what He requires of me: "forgiving each other, just as in Christ God forgave you" (Ephesians 4:32). Sometimes after a fight, I refused to forgive my husband because he refused to forgive me. Even though he did wrong, all he looked at was what I did. And I have to confess that's exactly what I often did—stayed blind to my part in the conflict.

These days, I'm determined to be the first one to obey God's command to forgive.

The Lord Gives Help to Forgive

Recently, memories of wrongs Randy had done to me invaded my mind. Once again anger and hurt rose up in me. I wanted to move on, but it seemed impossible. In the midst of my battle to forgive, God showed me pride led to my angry responses, excessive hurts, over-reactions, and bitterness time and time again in my marriage and in other relationships. Even though I felt wronged and hurt, I hurt others by my reaction. Pride blocked the forgiveness God wanted to flow to me and through me. And, because of pride, I violated my quest to love unconditionally. Instead of letting love lead, I allowed anger and hurt to take over.

God showed me forgiveness was the answer to bringing up my husband's sin over and over. One way I can keep silent about my husband's past failures, faults, and foibles is to pour them out to the Lord. To bring them up to Randy again and again not only doesn't help, but instead causes him discouragement. Forgiving my father made a huge difference in forgiveness toward my husband. The repair of my relationship with my dad came first and then came the healing of my marriage.

A while ago I read this: "In forgiving we give up demands for perfect behavior, perfect justice, perfect resolution, perfect retribution. All we can ask is genuine repentance of ourself and of the other. In forgiving we give up the angry picture of the wrongdoer. We put aside the view of the other as an unworthy, unacceptable, unforgivable offender. In forgiving we lay aside the view of ourselves as righteous and the other as totally unrighteous, and we begin to experience the truth that we are both fallible humans in need of being forgiven." (David Augsburger, *The Freedom of Forgiveness*, Moody Press, Chicago, IL 1970, page 46)

Forgiveness doesn't mean I remain silent when my husband hurts me. Recently in counseling Randy told the counselor how happy our marriage became when he did his own thing through isolation with the computer and the TV and how he "let me" do my own thing with writing and travels to visit relatives and attendance at most events by myself. He described it as his happy time. I viewed it as a period of dismal disconnection, and I felt sad and hurt that he withdrew from me. We lived then as little more than roommates. The problem worsened because I didn't communicate this to Randy at the time. Lack of communication caused unforgiveness to spring up in me when my husband didn't even know he hurt me.

Too often I said the words, "Lord, I can't forgive." Now I know this truth: I can go to God and ask Him to give me a willing heart. Then He takes my willingness, which is the same as humility, and pours His grace on it.

I found this on a little card in my notes about forgiveness. "Forgiveness isn't easy; it's impossible without His grace." God is generous to give me all the grace I need to forgive my husband and continue to love him through every difficult day.

Lord, open my eyes to the effects of unforgiveness on our marriage. Let Your gift of mercy flow to me and through me to my husband. In Jesus' name. Amen.

Part XII

The Role of My Husband's Cheerleader

Love… rejoices with the truth [when right and truth prevail]. —1 Corinthians 13:4-6 AMP

Many marriages would be better
if the husband and the wife clearly understood that
they are on the same side." —Zig Ziglar

Chapter 33

Learning to Encourage

Scores of people say to me, "Emma, you encourage me so much."

Whether through words of comfort in a note, a prayer, or a story of God's faithfulness, the Lord uses me to bring words to lift people's spirits. So why do I struggle to be an encourager to my husband?

Battle With Discouragement

Discouragement prevents my desire to encourage Randy. Too often, he delivered cruel words to me due to his own battles. Also, when he felt inadequate as a husband, he chose to point out angrily my flaws in an effort to help himself feel better. It seems we both fell into that negative habit, so instead of obedience to God's instruction of "build one another up," we found ourselves entangled in the trap of cut-downs.

The role of cheerleader to my husband proved difficult for me. How does one cheer for the athlete who seems to play for the other team (Satan and his cohorts)? As I sought the Lord with this question, the truth I received seemed clear: He does not play for the other side, but faces deceit by them. Also, he distrusts his teammates (namely me) because of hurts suffered in the past from other fellow team members (his family and friends who betrayed him).

When Randy wanders from the Lord's will and ways, and sins against me and our marriage, I now choose to see him as a prisoner of war. If I view my husband as a brainwashed captive, I become diligent to pray for the Lord to set him free and teach me to encourage him with truth.

I fail as an encourager when I deliver truth with irritability and in a strident manner instead of with love and gentleness.

See What My Husband Does Right

To build up my husband challenges me because I tend to criticize due to lack of encouragement as a child. But as I seek the Lord, He shows me how to accomplish this task.

I confess I take for granted what Randy does right. I slip into an attitude of, "Well, he's supposed to do these tasks as a husband."

When Randy rebels against God, I convince myself if I give my prodigal husband encouragement, he'll stay on the wrong path. But I discovered I can encourage him in the areas where he follows God. I rejoice out loud when my husband still gives a tithe to the church even when he withdraws from God in other ways.

The Battle With Criticism

Both Randy and I battle the problem of criticism. We each habitually point out flaws and failures, which hurts our relationship. One day, when I listened to the critical words which poured from my mouth, I decided to put an end to them. But then I noticed Randy often criticized me; therefore my criticism of him came as a defensive move. Later, I found out he felt the same way. He saw many of my comments as criticism that I viewed otherwise.

If I asked a question about a household item that needed repair, he viewed it as criticism. I inquired where I could find a tool, and he labelled it criticism. One day when I asked an innocent question he said, "You're trying to declare me inadequate."

"My husband would take almost everything, good or bad, that I said as an attack upon him. I was afraid to say anything," one wife reported to me.

I knew exactly how she felt.

"I don't criticize you any more than I criticize myself," Randy told me one day. That statement brought me to the realization: when I encourage my husband by a firm focus on what's good and right about him, I help to tip the scales away from the condemnation that torments his soul. I saw how easily I stayed fixated on outer actions and failed to take a look at the heart of my husband.

My husband's good qualities include: a hard worker, a devoted father, an excellent provider, a committed husband (he hasn't walked away yet), someone who desires to do the right thing, a loving friend to many, a beloved child of God, and the list goes on. I learned to remind my husband of his good qualities rather than point out what he does wrong.

Shame and Criticism

As I pondered our problem with criticism, as well as Randy's ongoing negativity toward me because I'm female, I saw that underneath our criticism lay a problem with shame.

In her book, *Christian Men Who Hate Women; Healing Hurting Relationships*, Dr. Margaret J. Rinck writes: "a shame state leads to lifestyle shame responses such as: hiding our weaknesses, blaming others, projecting our shame on others, defensiveness, becoming critical of self and others, perfectionism, works-orientation, fear of closeness…, power/control tactics, judgmental behavior…" (Zondervan 1990, page 95)

Randy and I both battle these shame responses in our lives. When I embrace this truth, I free myself to pray we will each take our shame to the cross and leave it there, so we can encourage one another. But even if Randy won't do that, I can choose to.

Words of Encouragement

Here are words of encouragement that came forth naturally, or rather supernaturally, as I asked God how to encourage my husband:

- I feel blessed to have a husband who provides so well financially for his family.
- Your generosity to others inspires me.
- I can tell by your tears you possess a compassionate heart.

I notice when I express gratitude to my husband for his thoughtfulness he sees it as encouragement, i.e., "You cooked dinner! Thank you, honey." "Thank you for your willingness to watch movies with me that I want to see," and "Thank you for this cheese you bought. I appreciate you remembered how much I like it."

Chapter 34

When My Husband Backslides

Repeatedly, I prayed for my husband to become a more godly man. For a time he moved in that direction. He sought God with all of his heart, and often studied the Word. He displayed profound insights in regard to Scripture, and attended what our church called, "a deep study" of the Bible and expressed excitement about what he learned there. The teacher took me aside and told me, "I studied the Bible for years and know Greek and Hebrew, and yet your husband comes up with amazing insights about the Bible."

During those days, encouragement proved easy. Randy loved the seeker's path, which thrilled me. But when hard times hit his business, and life failed to unfold in line with his plan, he backed away from God and stopped his wholehearted pursuit of Him. He returned to his pursuit of the pleasures of this world for satisfaction.

At first, I judged him for this, but I see I also fight this battle on a regular basis. I simply don't stay away as long. A crisis similar to my husband's came when our children turned away from the Lord, while my number one goal as a mother, and even as a Christian, centered on raising godly children. My temptation to withdraw from all Christian fellowship grew. It hurt too much when people asked, "How are your daughters?" or told me about the godly pursuits of their children. Certainly it stung my husband when people asked, "How's your business?" and his answer boiled down to, "my business failed."

Become His Wonderful Encourager

Recently, a friend spoke words to me which encouraged my soul. She called me "beautiful" and "precious" and "lovely in God's sight." She added more words which gave me courage to move forward with ministries God called me to. She urged me to minister to my husband, no matter how he treated me.

I have many other faithful friends who offer me words of encouragement on a regular basis.

Afterward I thought, *does Randy have any wonderful encouragers like that in his life?* Yes, some relatives and old friends who live in other states build him up, but in his everyday life, since he lives the life of a loner in his retirement, he doesn't receive uplifting words consistently, like I do.

Because Randy chooses to be a loner, on many days I serve as the only encourager he encounters. Too often, I fail to fully embrace that role.

Don't Let His Anger Stop Encouragement

I tend to cut off words of encouragement to my husband when he dumps his anger on me. Early in our marriage, Randy consistently exhibited anger, which discouraged me.

At first, I viewed him as a monster who wanted to destroy my soul. But as I prayed about how God saw him, I realized he was like a frightened child, (just like my dad), which helped me.

Now, counter to my natural inclination to withdraw, lash out, or take to heart his hurtful words when he gets angry, I choose instead to speak encouraging words—even when he erupts with harsh, critical words, which often magnify my false "not good enough" belief from childhood.

In the past, Randy repeatedly expressed anger over money. He ranted, "Where did all the money go?" If I couldn't remember every penny I spent, he appeared about to panic. I argued about these money issues, which only caused him to shout louder. When I asked God to show me why, He gave me this truth: I failed to address the fear he had—the fear of failure as a provider.

These days, if he starts to get upset about money, I realize the core of the problem centers not on me, but on his battle with fear. Then I say something to calm the fear—words to encourage—rather than attempt to argue against the anger and/or defend myself.

I say, "Honey, you excel at the role of excellent provider. And I celebrate God's faithfulness to bless us financially over all these years. I don't think He'll stop now."

When I remember Randy's anger centers on his fear, I feel free to encourage. If I focus only on the anger, I want to fight back, and often respond angrily with harsh words of my own, instead of with words of encouragement.

Recently as I refrained from an angry response in regard to Randy's explosion about a money issue, he calmed quickly and admitted, "I'm sorry I panicked."

I learned over time to ask my husband or the Lord what my husband fears at the moment. Then I find ways to encourage him in that area. Also, when I feel discouraged, and my husband cannot, because of his woundedness, encourage me, I can go to the Lord and receive the encouragement I need.

Battling Wrongdoing With Truth

God calls me to be an encourager instead of a person quick to point out errors in my husband. In 1 Corinthians 13:6 I read that love "Rejoiceth not in iniquity, but rejoiceth in the truth;" (KJV). I confess I rejoiced at times over my husband's wrongdoing, in the sense that I felt smug in my attitude of "I'm so much better than him." Instead, I need to rejoice in these truths:

- He and I both are sinners with a God who wants to lavish us with His grace. (God reminds me often: "There but for My grace, go you.")
- God loves us both equally and does not see one or the other as better. In fact, God sees us as one (See Mark 10:8).
- Because of the sacrificial death of Jesus, we are both saved from hell.

As I thought about truth in regard to my husband's battles in life, God showed me the following:

- Sin area of porn:Truth—Randy longs to do the right thing. The spirit is willing, but the flesh is weak.
- Sin area of anger: Truth—Randy exhibits a tender and compassionate heart, but fears take over and anger is the result. Truth—Instead of labeling my husband as an angry or mean man, I can choose to see him as the loving, compassionate man he is, whose fears often lead to anger.
- Sin area of becoming self-absorbed with the TV or computer, completely tuning out the world, including his family: Truth—when with his family, Randy is loving and kind, and he cares deeply about his extended

family and friends. By his own words, he uses TV and the computer to help with depression and anxiety. (I tend to use food.)

Chapter 35

Discovering Blocks To Encouragement

When I'm having a hard time speaking words of encouragement to Randy, I turn to Ephesians 4:29 to remind me of God's command to do so. "Do not let any unwholesome talk come out of your mouths, but only what is helpful for building others up according to their needs, that it may benefit those who listen."

God faithfully gives me the grace to speak "building-up" words to encourage my husband.

Perfectionism and Withholding Encouragement

As I thought of the difficulty I experienced when I desired to pass along encouragement to my husband, I realized how the perfectionism passed along from my family hindered me. My parents seemed to notice only what I did wrong, so naturally I repeated the error not only with my husband, but also with the children. One day, my youngest daughter said, "I never do anything right." Her statement surprised me since she was a sweet child who tried to obey. Then I realized my criticism, which I thought was constructive, discouraged her. God showed me the following points which helped me to notice what my children did correctly (they also apply to marriage.):

- Assess your expectations. Mine were often too high.
- Learn their strengths. I tended to focus on family members' weaknesses rather than their strengths.
- Be observant. Observing and accentuating the positive takes practice.
- Pass on what is right. Sometimes I think in my mind how special my husband is, but I don't say it to him, nor to others about him.

Husband Appreciation Challenge

God used a challenge from a radio show host to help me see how few encouraging words I said to Randy. Nancy DeMoss Wolgemuth on her radio show "Revive Our Hearts" urged listeners to embrace a 30 day Husband Appreciation Challenge. We were told to compliment and encourage our husbands every day for 30 days. About halfway through the challenge, during the time he was struggling with serious business and financial matters, apparently Randy thought my encouragement was born of worry and said, "Honey, you don't have to worry. I'm not going to kill myself."

Maintaining the Role of Encourager

These words recently challenged me: "People don't know how wonderful they are. Someone has to tell them." In marriage, that means I need to tell my spouse. Yes, it's acceptable to tell my husband what bothers me, but I don't need to repeat it a thousand times. When I can't seem to find anything to praise about Randy, I find I allowed unforgiveness to creep in, and I need to repent.

Though I don't approve of some of what Randy does, good qualities exist if I simply take time to dwell on them. Too often, I take for granted Randy's qualities such as a caring father, an excellent provider and money manager. He excels at fixing things, and he forgives quickly when I've blown it. Yet, I often find myself challenged to lavish genuine praise on him—to thank him for all he does for me and tell him how much he means to me.

At times, I fall back into critical wife instead of the encouraging wife, and I pray the Lord will help me not to stay there.

Ironically, I wanted very much to be a cheerleader as a teenager. I tried out, but failed to make the team. Yet God gives me the opportunity to cheer for a team—our marriage. I pray for grace to fully embrace that role.

Lord, help me pass along encouragement to my husband—even when I feel discouraged by what he says and does. Give me the grace not to lose heart, but to be tenderhearted toward the love of my life. In Jesus' name I pray. Amen.

Part XIII

The Faithful, Faith-filled Wife

Love...believes all things...
—1 Corinthians 13:7 AMP

FAITH = Fantastic Adventure In Trusting Him
—Corrie ten Boom

Chapter 36

Growing in Faith

When my older daughter, Suzanne, was around seven years old, our cat became ill. Riffy ate poorly, and his usual playful disposition disappeared. We took him to the vet numerous times, but the doctor couldn't figure out what ailed him. The cat's health worsened. One day, the vet announced that the only course was to put our cat to sleep.

In the midst of my preparation to talk and pray with Suzanne about saying goodbye to the cat, she proclaimed, "Riffy is my best friend, and I know God will make him well."

She called out to God that day to cure her cat, and she declared she didn't want him to go back to "that killing doctor."

Riffy regained his health. And the faith of my little child helped my own faith to grow. Things didn't "look" good for the cat, but Suzanne refused to care about that.

When I'm tempted to give up on our marriage, God repeatedly reminds me of His power as I turn to Him and say, "I do believe; help me overcome my unbelief!" (Mark 9:24). He intervenes—perhaps not the way I want—but He does act and repeatedly brings me back to the place of bold faith for my marriage and for my husband.

"Now faith is confidence in what we hope for and assurance about what we do not see," I read in Hebrews 11:1. I'm convicted of how much I need to grow in faith—especially when it comes to married life.

For years, I rarely felt confident in my hope for our marriage, or assured about what I did not see, unlike my daughter who expected God's intervention with all her heart.

Not long ago, I met a woman, Melissa, who maintained her faith for her marriage. She told me, when she and her husband suffered through difficulties, everyone told them to get a divorce—even her parents and in-laws. But she held to a stubborn faith and believed in God's intervention.

God delights in that kind of faith, where we live by faith, not by sight. (See 2 Corinthians 5:7)

Fear vs Faith

So many problems in our marriage center on our individual battles with fear—which originated in our childhoods. These fears erode our faith. I like what I read on the marquis at a church in our area, "Feeding your faith helps to starve your fears."

One day, I realized I possessed no power to get Randy to let go of his fears, but I could allow God to free me from mine. Whenever I lose my faith in our marriage, and it seems impossible to go on in the same house with Randy, I examine my emotions and recognize fears as the root cause. But as I turn to God, He delights to release me from fear. When I refuse to turn to God, fears take control. This describes where I've been too often.

What Am I Afraid Of?

Sometimes I want to pretend I've overcome all fears. Like seeds underground, some fears stay hidden. During trials and hardships, they resurface and try to choke the life from me and our marriage.

One day I asked myself, "What am I afraid of?" This is what came to mind:

Fear of rejection—especially from men.
Fear of failure.
Fear of feeling disconnected.

Behaviors in my husband often triggered these fears. I felt rejected when he became angry, a failure when he criticized, and disconnected when he withdrew. Instead of allowing my fears to rule, I chose to ask God to deliver me from these fears.

Seek the Lord to Deal with Fears.

When fears affect my faith, I cling to Psalm 34:4: "I sought the LORD, and he answered me; he delivered me from all my fears." Whenever fear rises up in me, I try to go to God and pray my way through it.

Another verse which helps me overcome fears is Psalm 56:3: "When I am afraid, I put my trust in you." Often, fears take over because I can't trust Randy. As I put my trust more fully in the Lord, fears dissolve.

Dealing with fears can take a lifetime. When fears take over, I can defeat them when I realize my fears—not my spouse—constitute the enemy of peace and intimacy in marriage.

God's Perfect Love Eradicates Fear

"...perfect love drives out fear..." states 1 John 4:18. When I put my love in action and allow God's love to flow to me and then through me—even when I feel terrified Randy will hurt me again—this helps eradicate fear, and my faith grows.

Another example of truth related to fear can be found in 2 Timothy 1:7: "For God did not give us a spirit of timidity or cowardice or fear, but [He has given us a spirit] of power and of love and of sound judgment and personal discipline [abilities that result in a calm, well-balanced mind and self-control]" (AMP).

Fear in the Storm

Whenever I think of my desire to become a faith-filled wife and determine to let go of fear about the latest crisis in our marriage, God reminds me of the story in Scripture when the disciples gave in to fear.

"One day Jesus said to his disciples, 'Let us go over to the other side of the lake.' So they got into a boat and set out. As they sailed, he fell asleep. A squall came down on the lake, so that the boat was being swamped, and they were in great danger. The disciples went and woke him, saying, 'Master, Master, we're going to drown!' He got up and rebuked the wind and the raging waters; the storm subsided, and all was calm. 'Where is your faith?' he asked his disciples…" (Luke 8:2-25).

What Jesus said to the disciples, He often speaks to me. Even though Jesus promises to get me to the other side of my battles, and Jesus remains on the marriage boat with us, sometimes my faith falters in the midst of storms. Jesus knew of these storms in our marriage even before my husband and I met, and He can help us through them—if I allow Him to.

Chapter 37

More About Dealing With Fear and Anxiety

I must deal with my fear and anxiety if I want to become a faith-filled wife. Not only do my husband's issues hurt our marriage, but so do my fears about them and my wrong reactions in connection to them.

When I hold on to fear, misery follows. When I hold firmly to my faith in God, joy springs up. One day I read this in a devotion a friend gave me: "Remember, the only place fear has to work is in the empty space where your faith should be. Fear is based on what you see and hear. Faith is based on knowing that God's Word is reliable, and that He promises 'good things' to those who believe Him for them!"

Depend on God Rather than Thoughts and Feelings

As I grow up in the Lord, my feelings no longer rule over me. My faith fails when I depend only on my emotions—especially fear. Recently, I wondered why the Word says to take only our thoughts captive and not feelings. "...we take captive every thought to make it obedient to Christ" (2 Corinthians 10:5). I realized my thought life generates those feelings. Once I gain control of my thoughts, then the feelings come in line.

The psalmist, David, expresses his feelings, but refuses to rely on them. He comes back to truth about God—who He is, what He's done, and what He promises to do. The psalms help me bring my thoughts and my feelings in line with truth.

When Husbands are Prodigals

I view my husband as a prodigal when he loses interest in the things of God and seems to possess a diminished sense of right and wrong. If I embrace my role as a faith-filled wife, I believe he will come home, but I don't demand it of him or of God. In the past, my frets and fears led me to try to drag him home against his will, or give up completely on his ever returning to the Lord.

Ruth Graham reminds me of a truth in her book *Prodigals and Those Who Love Them*. (Baker Books 1991, 1999) "We cannot convict of sin, create hunger and thirst after God or convert…But we can love them right where they are and continue to pray for their return."

I can relate to a woman quoted in Lee Strobel's book, *Surviving a Spiritual Mismatch in Marriage*. (Zondervan 2002) "I love to go to church and worship God and study the Bible and pray and participate in my small group, but he sort of just tolerates church. He isn't involved in any ministry. He doesn't talk a lot about spiritual matters. He seems content to be lukewarm in his faith—and it's creating more and more tension in our relationship." (page 207)

The author gives this counsel to those of us in the same state of affairs in our marriages:

"It is a far better approach to accentuate the positive and to sincerely and enthusiastically applaud whatever spiritual progress you see in your partner. Spouses have a tendency to become what their loved ones praise in them. Speaking gentle words of respect and encouragement, whether in private or in front of others, can be extremely influential in bringing about a desire for change." (Page 219)

Believing God

One key to a lifelong marriage and forever love lies in the maintenance of a vital connection to God, and a constant belief in what He says over what I see. It means I stay dedicated to His agenda rather than my own; I obey Him and seek to bring Him glory, rather than put myself at the center of my situation. It took me years to realize this remains the only course in marriage which truly succeeds.

Satan repeatedly tempts me to let go of God and try to work out my situation in my own strength. He attempts to convince me my ideas of straightening out my husband will work. And they do work—but only to make matters worse. Satan strives to dissolve my faith and get me to find a way out of my marriage, and a way out of loving like Jesus.

Cry Out To God

Wherever I turn when marriage difficulties hit, is where I place my faith whether it be God, friends, books, my own wisdom, worldly wisdom. As I grow in faith, I let go of vain refuges and allow God to be my refuge when stormy times threaten our marriage. Yes, He may then lead me to books or friends, but He remains in charge.

When my life ends on this earth, I want to appear before the Lord and hear Him say in regard to my faithfulness in spite of all my trials: "...Well done, good and faithful servant..." Matthew 25:23

Lord, help me continue to be a faithful, faith-filled wife even if it seems my husband is weak in his faith. Deliver me from my fears and help me keep my eyes on You. In Jesus' name I pray. Amen.

Part XIV

A Test of Endurance

Love bears all things [regardless of what comes]…
endures all things [without weakening].
—1 Corinthians 13:7 AMP

Great works are performed not by strength but by
perseverance. —Samuel Johnson

Chapter 38

Learning Endurance

Early in our marriage, Randy and I engaged in ugly fights which left us feeling battered and scarred. We both shouted angry words in the heat of the moment. We blamed each other for our outbursts. So often I thought to myself in those days, *I cannot endure a lifetime of this.*

And yet, we've made it to 43 years of marriage. Over the years, we learned to be more civil, with rare times when we fall off the wagon. I attribute this to the gift of endurance from the Lord, which He gave to both of us. He showed me these hard times won't kill me or our marriage, but they taught me what to avoid, and how to love my husband—in his most difficult moments and even when he hurts me deeply.

Endurance Defined

I ponder often the definition for endurance I wrote years ago in my Bible: "the quality that does not surrender to circumstances nor succumb when under pressure." I wrote it next to James 1:4 which states: "And let endurance have its perfect result and do a thorough work, so that you may be perfect and completely developed [in your faith], lacking in nothing"

(AMP). That's what I want, and as I determine to endure I will arrive at that point. Marriage serves as an excellent vehicle to allow endurance to do a thorough work on my soul.

Deal With Differences

Endurance becomes necessary to accept our differences and learn to be more flexible because of them. I remember a saying I heard once which proved to be a good one for me to embrace: "Blessed are the flexible, for they shall not be bent out of shape."

Angela Hunt writes about differences in her book, *Then Comes Marriage* (Zondervan 2001, coauthor Bill Myers): "Maybe the process of two becoming one wasn't something that happened through the magic of love, but through the process of learning...and bending. Of giving sometimes, and apologizing sometimes, and sometimes accepting that differences made life much more...challenging." (Kindle DX 74%/1204-7/Chapter Nine)

Part of endurance in marriage centers on acceptance of each other. This issue repeatedly arose when I tried to make my husband into someone else.

"I think you want to make me into one of your girlfriends," Randy said one day. It proved difficult, but necessary, to admit the truth of his statement.

Titles of some books on the subject remind me God made men and women different. *Men Are From Mars, Women Are From Venus: The Classic Guide to Understanding the Opposite Sex,* a secular book by John Gray, Ph.D. (© 1992 by J.G. Productions) and *Men Are Like Waffles; Women Are Like Spaghetti: Understanding and Delighting in Your Differences* (© 2001, Harvest House Publishers) by Christians Bill and Pam Farrel are two that come to mind. Randy and I attended the Love and Respect Conference presented by Emerson Eggerichs, author of

Love and Respect (Simon & Schuster © 2004) which opened our eyes to how men and women view life differently. Randy saw he often attempted to make me think and be like a man, and I realized again I got caught up in my attempts to make him be and think like a woman. As we discovered the differences between men and women, our attitudes and our marriage improved.

Focus on Giving, Not Getting

In her book, *How To Act Right When Your Spouse Acts Wrong*, (Waterbrook Press, 2001) Leslie Vernick writes: "Today we live in a culture that is more concerned with getting than giving. Over and over in my counseling sessions I hear spouses complain, 'My needs aren't being met in my marriage.' Dissatisfaction, anger, resentment, and bitterness are the mainstays in many homes because we go into marriage seeking what we can get out of it."

As I read her book, I realized doing the right thing when my husband isn't, is key to endurance in marriage. Leslie goes on to say: "Acting right when our spouse acts wrong will not necessarily guarantee a more satisfying marital relationship, although it often does. Acting right may not make our spouse turn around and change his or her ways or meet our needs, although it could. God says that we exert a powerful influence over others as we seek to lovingly interact with them...As we start learning how to act right when our spouse acts wrong, we will begin to see what God is doing to make us more like Him in the midst of marital difficulties. We will become able to look at the idiosyncratic differences of our spouse less problematically and learn how to respond wisely when wronged. Perhaps most important of all, learning to act right when our spouse acts wrong will force us to forage for a deeper relationship with Christ." (Kindle DX 5%/155-163/Introduction)

One area where it seemed I would not be able to endure was when my husband desired no physical or emotional intimacy with me. I felt hurt and alone. I discovered that as I drew near to the Lord during those times, intimacy with Him filled up every void I felt because of lack of intimacy with my husband. As I sought intimacy with the Lord as a priority, He restored intimacy with my husband.

Chapter 39

Never Give Up

I must never forget Satan's goal is to get me to give up. He even whispers such things into my mind. His plan focuses on destruction of my marriage. God's plan is to destroy the strongholds in my life, which helps to draw me away from the desire to desert my marriage.

When I feel trapped in the "I can't bear this anymore" desert, God encourages me to embrace the concept of Christ in me. When I cannot find an encouraging word or see a single worthwhile aspect of my marriage, it's because self, and not Christ shines through me.

As a runner, I run alongside other runners who encourage me. We each battle issues as we run—breathlessness, muscle fatigue, hurting feet—but we lift one another up with the attitude of, "We can complete this race." We help each other keep up the pace. When it comes to marriage, God brings good Christian friends beside me who also face difficulties. We encourage one another to endure every hardship and use it to bring glory to God.

As part of my enduring, I surround myself with people who believe in the permanence of marriage. Sometimes they can be difficult to find. I avoid men-haters and the bitter divorced—even in the body of Christ.

Beware of those who say, "You shouldn't have to endure that." God calls me to endure.

When I Hit the Wall

From marathoners I've heard of a phenomenon called "hitting the wall." Here's how one runner describes it: "You're in the middle of a run when things start to fall apart. Your legs feel like concrete, your breathing grows labored, your strides turn into a shuffle. Negative thoughts flood your mind, and the urge to quit becomes overwhelming." Marriage can feel like a marathon; we can experience similar problems on the mental, emotional and spiritual level—especially the part about negative thoughts and the urge to quit.

Some of the suggestions to help runners overcome "hitting the wall" can also help in marriage: Take your mind off of your running and think of other things. Look to the crowd for support. One runner I know reached the wall, and she was certain she couldn't go on. Suddenly a spectator—a stranger—came out from the crowd and hugged her. She was able to continue and finished the race. Even a thumbs up can help. Also, it's important to take care of your body before and during the race, i.e., staying hydrated. Even in marriage, physiological needs wear us out, like lack of sleep or overworking at our jobs which wears out our bodies. Staying in the Word offers us living water for our spirits to continue on in the race called marriage.

Acts 20:24 reminds me of the race I run for the Lord: "However, I consider my life worth nothing to me, my only aim is to finish the race and complete the task the Lord Jesus has given me—the task of testifying to the good news of God's grace." As

I read that verse, I realized when I stay married and keep loving my husband through hard times, I testify to God's grace.

When I'm Weary

Galatians 6:9 states: "Let us not become weary in doing good, for at the proper time we will reap a harvest if we do not give up." When I focus on what Randy does wrong rather than on what he does right, it wears me out. Occasionally when I slip back into *he's-the-enemy* coupled with *I-can't-endure-this* thinking, Randy will say, "Honey, you forgot again; we're a team." I appreciate his reminder, because I forget it all too often. We're partners working together to build a strong union and working against the enemy who remains bent on the destruction of our marriage. God has kept the promise in Galatians 6:9, I am reaping a harvest because I did not give up on doing good in my marriage.

God Carries Us

My self-talk says, "I can't endure this anymore." The good news is I don't have to. God will bear me up and carry me through hard times. Too often I look to my husband to do that; however, he's not able to. But here's what God promises He will do for me as I lean on Him: "Praise be to the Lord, to God our Savior, who daily bears our burdens" (Psalm 68:19).

I do not have to endure alone.

Lord, give me grace today to endure hardships in our marriage. Then when people ask, "How did you do it?" I can point them to You. In Jesus' name I pray. Amen.

Part XV

Holding On To Hope

Love…hopes all things [remaining steadfast
during difficult times]…
—1 Corinthians 13:7 AMP

When you say that a situation or a person is hopeless,
you are slamming the door in the face of God.
—Charles L. Allen

Chapter 40

Putting My Hope In God

One day I wrote down some of what I hoped for in regard to our marriage:

> I hope my husband changes.

> I hope my husband meets my needs.

> I hope for Randy to embrace deliverance.

> I hope Randy becomes all God called him to be.

> I hope Randy becomes an excellent spiritual leader for our family.

I reread this list, and saw God wasn't at the center of my hopes.

As I studied the Word and looked up verses about hope, I gradually understood the error of placing my hope in my husband, a fallible man who failed often. I needed to put my hope in God. When I put my hope in Him and His unfailing love for me, I found myself more joyful, with fewer ups and downs in my emotional life in regard to marriage.

Waiting, Hoping, Enduring

Once I took my mind off feeling hopeless because my husband didn't express his love to me in the way I wanted to be loved, I determined to learn to truly love him. As I studied 1 Corinthians 13 in an effort to learn how to do this, I discovered three of the "love is" statements—"Love is patient," "love hopes all things," and "love endures all things"—are tied together.

Isaiah 40:31 centers on waiting, hoping and enduring. While many versions give promises to "those who wait upon the Lord" others like the NIV say: "those who hope in the Lord." The Amplified Bible connects the waiting and the hoping. "But those who wait for the LORD [who expect, look for, and hope in Him] will gain new strength and renew their power; they will lift their wings and [and rise up close to God] like eagles [rising toward the sun]; they will run and not become weary, they will walk and not grow tired."

As I saw "the wait-hope-endure interconnection," I realized when I made statements like "I'm sick of waiting for something good to happen," or "I just can't endure this anymore," this led to hopelessness and showed I once again shifted my focus to my husband changing, instead of keeping it on the Lord.

Putting My Hope in the Lord

On the way to a counseling session one day, my husband accused me: "You have lost hope in me." After I thought about it for a few minutes, I realized when I put my hope in him, it created a problem.

When I feel overwhelmed by disappointments—typically based on something other than what I expected, I easily give in to hopelessness, especially when I expect God to do something extraordinary in my marriage when I pray, but instead it seems He does nothing. As I put my hope in God, marital disappointments no longer overwhelm me. Here's what Romans 5:5 says about the matter: "...hope [in God's promises] never disappoints us, because God's love has been abundantly poured out within our hearts through the Holy Spirit who was given to us." (AMP)

John Koessler writes in his book, *The Surprising Grace of Disappointment; Finding Hope When God Seems to Fail Us*, (Moody 2013) "Expectation, as important as it is when it comes to God, is not always a reflection of faith. Sometimes expectation is a sign of arrogance. There is a world of difference between a confident request and a demand....When it comes to God, we have no right to command, much less make demands of Him. We are at His beck and call. He is not at ours."

This writer convicted me further as to why I often felt hopeless: "...we can grow irritated with Jesus when He seems unresponsive to our requests. We appreciate the encouragement of His Word, but would like something more substantial. Specifically, we want Him to get with the program—our program—and comply with the agenda we have set for Him. But the God who hears us when we cry also acts in His own time and in His own way. He is a God who makes promises. But He is also the one who determines how He will keep them. This is the chief difference between faith and presumption. Faith and presumption both expect something from God. Presumption wants to call the shots. Faith bows the knee." (pages 40-41)

Chapter 41

Avenues of Hope

During hard times, it's essential to have a good support system. It's not enough merely to fellowship with other Christians. I need women of faith to help me maintain a godly perspective and assist me in keeping hope alive in hard times.

In my most difficult times, I looked for people who said, "There's hope for your marriage—no matter what struggles you're going through." Often, I found such people in short supply in my home church, where there seemed to be an epidemic of divorce.

But I did find good support elsewhere—in interdenominational Bible studies, in friendships with godly, faith-filled, women who hear God's voice, and in listening to radio shows with a high view of marriage. On some occasions, after a fight, one of these programs brought exactly what I needed to bring my focus into proper perspective. Someone knew what I was going through. I wasn't alone, and what Randy and I faced was a common problem.

I also found hope with godly counselors who helped me change my perspective on marriage and brought me back to this truth: "It's not all about me."

Avoid Isolation

When I'm battling hopelessness, I encounter the temptation to isolate myself, as I once did for a time. I didn't want to go to church or my Bible study. I determined I didn't want anyone to know what I was going through—a marriage hanging by a thread.

In her book, *Unquenchable; Grow A Wildfire Faith,* Carol Kent says, to those going through any trial including those in marriage: "we often cut ourselves off from fellow Christians and in so doing we extricate ourselves from the very sources necessary to ignite and sustain the fire of revival...In community, we learn we are not alone, because not only do others demonstrate genuine care; they have also experienced like circumstances, and from this we take hope." (Kindle DX 12%/387 & 390/Chapter One)

As I determined, in those early times of isolation, to keep attending church and return to my Bible study, I learned not to keep my marital pain a secret. I allowed myself to cry in front of others. When I was honest some people showed discomfort, but others offered godly counsel, hugs, prayers, tears, and stories about their own pain and marital difficulties as well as God's intervention.

But I need to be careful who I listen to in church settings. Many people encourage leaving a difficult marriage. However, as God revived our marriage, I felt led to spend time giving hope to wives who come to me with their hopelessness. God continues to keep me involved in that unofficial ministry.

Overcoming Negative Self-talk

The book, *Spiritual Depression; It's Causes and Its Cures,* (Wm B Eerdmans 2003, 1965) by D Martyn Lloyd-Jones helped me tremendously with the monster of negative self-talk. The author asks: "Have you realized that most of the unhappiness in life is due to the fact that you are listening to yourself instead of talking to yourself? Take those thoughts that come to you the moment you wake up in the morning. You have not originated them, but they start talking to you, they bring back the problems of yesterday, etc. Somebody is talking. Who is talking to you? ...this self of ours, this other man within us, has got to be handled. Do not listen to him; upbraid him; exhort him; encourage him; remind him of what you know, instead of listening placidly to him and allowing him to drag you down and depress you. For that is what he will always do if you allow him to be in control." (pages 20-21)

I reread that quote and put in "woman" and "her." I read it many times over and began to follow the instructions. They changed my life, my marriage, and helped renew my hope.

Hope and A Future

A favorite verse I like to recite is Jeremiah 29:11: "'For I know the plans I have for you,' declares the LORD, 'plans to prosper you and not to harm you, plans to give you hope and a future.'" For years I failed to apply it to my marriage. But these days when I feel I'm losing hope, I look at the verse. This is how I pray that verse for my life with Randy: "I praise You, Lord, that You know the plans You have for me and Randy as a couple—plans to prosper us and not to harm us. Plans to give us a future and a hope."

Not long ago God gave me an insight on this verse: Satan has a plan too. If Satan had a verse of his own it would read like this: "I know the plans I have for your marriage, plans to keep it from prospering and plans to harm you. Plans to cause you to believe you have no future in this relationship, and there is no hope for you and Randy and your life together." I discovered if I'm feeling hopeless and that "the love is gone," I know from where those thoughts arise. Certainly not from the Lord.

Holding to God's Promises

God gave me this acronym for hope: Holding Onto Promises Expectantly—not my husband's promises, but God's. My husband makes promises and breaks them. I do the same to him at times. Only God is the perfect promise-keeper. If I hold to my husband's promises, I lose hope. As I hold to God's promises, my hope soars.

Delving deeply into God's Word restores me to peace and to hope as I trust in Him and realize my husband cannot be trusted. None of us can. But the good news is: God can be trusted. He, not my husband, is my Rock, and if I hold to that and to Him, I will have hope.

Lord, I praise You that You are my hope, and You can rescue me from the pit of hopelessness. Help me to stop hoping in my husband. Let me place my hope fully in You. In Jesus' name I pray. Amen.

Part XVI

Remain in His Love

If you keep my commands,
you will remain in my love…—John 15:10

An older couple was asked, "How did you manage
to stay together for so long?" Their answer was, "It's
simple, really. We are from a time where if something
was broken, we fix it, not throw it away." From poster
on Facebook —Source unknown.

Chapter 42

Healing My Broken Heart

Not long ago, I went to a healing class at a friend's house. One lady there gave her testimony about what she saw in her mind's eye when she invited Jesus into her crisis of cruel rejections from her parents, and later, from her husband and children.

She saw Jesus in a white room where lockers lined the wall. In each locker lay a broken heart—all hers—one for each heart-breaking event in her life. In this vision, she opened each locker and handed the broken heart to Jesus. He, in turn, took each damaged heart and put it into His heart.

Too often in my marriage, instead of going to Jesus, I tried to heal my own broken heart or demanded my husband do so. This never works, and often results in the temptation to fantasize about finding another husband who will somehow heal my broken heart. Some days I thought *maybe my husband will die, and then I'll be free to find a husband who has the key to healing my broken heart.* Other times, I withdrew from my spouse, saying, "I don't want him to break my heart any further."

God's solution differs. He wants to heal our broken hearts, so He can use us to heal the brokenness in our husband's heart—not with our own love, but with His love flowing through us.

Only God Heals Broken Hearts

Whenever I felt, "I have a broken heart in this marriage," I clung to this verse: "He heals the brokenhearted and binds up their wounds" (Psalm 147:3).

God doesn't give that responsibility to our husbands. Nor does it give it to our friends. He doesn't say Husband Number Two or three or even Husband Number Seven (a lucky number, after all), will complete the task. According to the Scripture above, He is the only One who can. When I contemplate the fragile nature of my own heart and how easily it shatters, and I think of all the broken hearts around the world, this promise seems incredible.

My broken heart didn't start in my marriage. It began to break long before that. Yet I wrongly expected my husband to heal it. And for years I often slipped back into that error. When he failed to do "his job," or when he added to my hurts and heartaches, I felt devastated and unloved. My unrealistic expectation centered on human beings to fix my broken heart. The hard truth came when I realized I could expect only hurt from my husband since hurt people hurt people. As Kim Sadler, a Daytona Beach counselor tells her clients: "Brokenness cannot fix brokenness."

The Remedy

The solution is to remain in God's love.

In John 15:1-2, Jesus says, "I am the true vine, and my Father is the gardener. He cuts off every branch in me that bears no fruit, while every branch that does bear fruit he prunes so that it will be even more fruitful..."

He goes on to say, in verses 4 and 5: "Remain in me, as I also remain in you. No branch can bear fruit by itself; it must remain

184

in the vine. Neither can you bear fruit unless you remain in me. I am the vine; you are the branches. If you remain in me and I in you, you will bear much fruit; apart from me you can do nothing."

As I read this, I like to replace the word fruit with "love" and apply it to loving my husband, since Galatians 5:22 says, "The fruit of the Spirit is love..." One radio show host said that every word following the word love in that verse is just an aspect of love. That does seem to be true.

So here's how I read those verses to help me grow in loving like Jesus: "He cuts off every branch in me that bears no love, while every branch that does bear love, he prunes so that it will be even more love-producing. Remain in me, as I also remain in you. No branch can be loving by itself; it must remain in the vine. Neither can you as a wife love unless you remain in me. I am the vine; you are the branch. If you remain in me, and I in you, you will love much, apart from me you cannot love at all."

In other words, if I want to love my husband, I must stay attached to the source of love—Jesus. The way to stay attached—to remain in Him and in His love—is through obedience. "If you keep my commands, you will remain in my love, just as I have kept my Father's commands and remain in his love" (John 15:10)

Abiding In Christ

To remain in God's love, I must abide in Christ. The enemy tries to lure me away from God and from abiding in Him, from allowing His love to flow through me to my husband. Compared to His limitless, endless love, mine is meager and far too limited. My love reacts negatively to circumstances. His does not. I cannot love my husband for a lifetime if I depend only on my own feelings of love or stay disconnected from the Lord.

God's love flowing through me makes the difference, and before it flows through me, His love first flows to me and heals my broken heart. Then it flows to my husband to help heal his.

Chapter 43

Abandonment to God

In order to abide in the Lord, I must abandon myself to Him, and, to do that, I must first abandon worldliness and my own individual desires. Only as I abandon myself to God, and stay dedicated to His agenda, rather than my own, do I remain in His love.

I want to abandon myself to Him, so I can love others, especially my husband, more completely. I desire to stop asking questions—to stop looking at "What's in this for me?" especially within my marriage. I desire boldness in living for Him and loving like Him. Yet a part of me shrinks in horror from that course. I realize I still fear being hurt; I fear losing my walls of self-protection. But Jesus did exactly that when He came to this earth.

How I long to live out Romans 12:1: "Therefore, I urge you, brothers and sisters, in view of God's mercy, to offer your bodies as a living sacrifice, holy and pleasing to God—this is your true and proper worship." Lately I pray, "Lord, help me to truly and fully abandon to You." Abandonment equals surrender. As I surrender to God, His love flows to me. When I seek my own course—my will and my way—the flow becomes dammed off.

Relapse in Marriage

It's easy to fall back into my goal of pursuing perfect love from my husband, rather than "being a loving wife." Relapse happens when I choose not to remain in God's love or in a state of surrender, but, instead, side with the enemy and his plan for me to become self-absorbed.

When in the midst of a relapse, I give in to negative emotions, become irritable, hurl criticisms, make demands. I stop doing the following: "In your relationships with one another, have the same mindset as Christ Jesus…" (Philippians 2:5) and "take captive every thought to make it obedient to Christ" (2 Corinthians 10:5). Instead, I let my thoughts and emotions lead the way. I fail to keep my eyes on Jesus.

Sometimes I feel exasperated because I decide I'm the one who holds our marriage together, and I'm failing at the endeavor. I forget what the Word of God says in Colossians 1:17 "…in him all things hold together." I praise God for the many times He intervenes and restores me when I fall into a state of relapse.

Chapter 44

Keeping Love Alive

The purpose of marriage is to bring God glory. I accomplish this when I love my husband as Christ loves me and when I allow my marriage to present a picture of Christ's love. This is not dependent on my husband. Even when I don't feel loved, and even if my spouse fails to show love because of his own hurts, I can love him unconditionally—the way God loves me. Beverly and Tom Rogers write in their book, *Soul-Healing Love,* "It is against human nature to give unconditionally. We humans tend to give to get. Christ's directive to love our enemies and bless those who hurt us, to turn the other cheek, goes against our very structure. How can we care for those who do not care about us? How indeed, can we care for our mates when we perceive them as uncaring, or even enemies? This is where we need God's divine help. We need to call on his unconditionally loving nature to enable us to actualize the part of ourselves that is most Christ-like. Christ then becomes the inspiration to transcend our humanity and follow his example. The solution to our human condition in marriage is simple. It is to love our mate as Christ first loved us. Remember, it is simple, not easy. Even with Christ's loving example to guide us, it is still hard for most Christian couples to move beyond the typical deal-making, tit-for-tat marriages that we are used to." (Resource Publications, Inc, San Jose, California, ©1998, page 168)

How do I love unconditionally—like my Lord loves me? John 8:31 states "...abide in My word [continually obeying My teachings and living in accordance with them]..." (AMP). I need to confess that I tend to fall short of this command and even resist it stubbornly.

How grateful I am that Jesus maintained love for God's people to the end. He didn't become fed up with the human race as He experienced the pettiness and the blatant sin that was so much a part of life on planet earth. He didn't give up on the people of earth the way we want to give up on the person we have pledged to love for the rest of our lives.

Jesus remained in the Father's love, and demonstrated that love on the cross when He died for my sin, for the sin of my husband, and for the sin of every human being. God desires I demonstrate that kind of love toward others—the love which says, "I will love you through everything."

I Take A Look Back

This year I celebrate 41 years as a Christian. I remember vividly the moment in my car 41 years ago when I said "yes" to Jesus as my Savior and "yes" to my husband's question, "Can't Jesus heal this marriage?" Jesus performed miraculous wonders in healing my soul. He healed our marriage and made it better than I ever dreamed it could be. Yes, we still have problems. Yes, we engage in battles at times, but our love for each other and for the Lord grows deeper with each passing year. How grateful I am to my husband for the question He asked that day, and to the Lord for convincing me the answer is and will always be "yes."

God gave me the following promise during the past several years, which I cling to as He fulfills it: "The best is yet to come."

My husband and I both look forward to growing old together. I can't help but think of Robert Browning's line of poetry: "Grow old along with me! The best is yet to be…"

Lord, Help me stay connected to You—to abide in You— so Your love will flow freely. May Your love remain in my heart and overflow to my husband for the rest of our lives together. In Jesus' name I pray. Amen.

Appendix #1

"Reasons To Stay Married"

Note: This was first published in the October 1997 issue of *Light and Life* magazine.

Before long Randy and I expect to celebrate our 25th wedding anniversary. Married life hasn't been easy. We both entered our marriage wounded, and too often we wounded one another. To go the way of the world and consult a lawyer, instead of the Lord, sorely tempted me. But every time we cried out to God, He gave only one answer "Stay married. Today we are reaping the blessings of obedience.

After asking the "Why did you divorce?" question many times over, I became convinced the reason Christians decide to divorce is because, most often, they believe lies—many of the same lies I was tempted to believe. Also, they are not well acquainted with the truths of the Scriptures—the weapon God has given us to combat those lies.

The following are excuses people have given for divorce, and some I have entertained, coupled with truth from Scripture. Even if you divorced because you, or your ex-spouse, or both embraced lies in the past, there is still great benefit in embracing truth right where you are.

Man's Lies	God's Truth
It was an impossible situation.	…all things are possible with God. Mark 10:27
I didn't have the strength to go on.	I can do all this through him who gives me strength. Philippians 4:13
God told me to get a divorce.	"For I hate divorce," says the LORD… Malachi 2:16 AMP
I have done everything in my power to get this marriage to work.	"Not by might, nor by power, but by my Spirit," says the LORD Almighty. Zechariah 4:6 NIV
I tried to fix things—stitch things together, but it didn't work.	…In him all things hold together. Colossians 1:17
I couldn't respect my husband/ wife.	Show respect for all people [treat them honorably]… Peter 2:17 AMP
I had to protect my sanity.	You are my hiding place; you will protect me from trouble and surround me with songs of deliverance. Psalm 32:7 NIV
Divorce was the only way.	And yet I will show you a still more excellent way [one of the choicest graces and the highest of them all: unselfish love]. I Corinthians 12:31 AMP
It was my last chance for happiness.	…blessed (happy, prosperous, to be admired) is he who trusts [confidently] in the Lord. Proverbs 16:20 AMP

The Lord brought another person into my life; my heart tells me that he/she's the only one for me.	The heart is deceitful above all things... Jeremiah 17:9 NIV
I couldn't bear it anymore.	Bear with each other and forgive one another if any of you has a grievance against someone. Colossians 3:13 NIV
We were constantly at war.	For our struggle is not against flesh and blood, but against the rulers, against the authorities, against the powers of this dark world and against the spiritual forces of evil in the heavenly realms. Ephesians 6:12 NIV
What my husband/wife did was unforgivable.	Forgive as the Lord forgave you. Colossians 3:13 NIV
My husband/wife didn't meet my needs.	And my God will meet all your needs according to the riches of his glory in Christ Jesus. Philippians 4:19 NIV
I hurt too much.	LORD, who may dwell in your sacred tent? ...who keeps an oath even when it hurts. Psalm 15:1,4 NIV
My lawyer (pastor, counselor) told me it would be the best thing.	I will instruct you and teach you in the way you should go... Psalms 32:8
Our problems were too hard to solve.	Is anything too hard for the LORD? Genesis 18:14
I couldn't wait any longer for my husband/wife to change.	Wait for the LORD; be strong and take heart and wait for the LORD. Psalms 27:14

I just needed to be free.	Then you will know the truth, and the truth will set you free. John 8:32
I thought divorce was the best choice.	I have spread out My hands all the day long to a rebellious and stubborn people, who walk in the way that is not good, [following] after their own thoughts and intentions. Isaiah 65:2 (AMP)
I just knew it was the right thing to do.	There is a way that appears to be right, but in the end it leads to death. Proverbs 14:12
I talked and talked, and he wouldn't listen.	...they may be won over without words by the behavior of their wives, when they see the purity and reverence of your lives. I Peter 3:1-2
There was no help for my marriage.	God is our refuge and strength, an ever-present help in trouble. Psalms 46:1
I couldn't trust my spouse.	Trust in the LORD with all your heart... Proverbs 3:5
My spouse said such cruel things to me.	Whoever dwells in the shelter of the Most High...will not fear the terror of night, nor the arrow that flies by day. Psalms 91:1,5
I didn't love him/her anymore.	Love never fails [it never fades nor ends]. I Corinthians 13:8 (AMP)
I was empty. I had nothing left in me to go on in the marriage.	...Open wide your mouth and I will fill it. Psalms 81:10

Divorce was my only way to be delivered.	The LORD is my rock, my fortress and my deliverer... Psalms 18:2
I felt like I was dying inside.	I die daily [I face death and die to self]. I Corinthians 15:31 (AMP)
There was no hope for our marriage.	May the God of hope fill you with all joy and peace as you trust in him, so that you may overflow with hope by the power of the Holy Spirit. Romans 15:13

The next time one of these lies—or others—tempt you, don't turn to a friend who's divorced, or the latest books which attempt to give Christians biblical loopholes for divorce. Turn to God and to His Word—not just for an answer for your current marriage crisis, but to build an intimate relationship with Him. He will make you into the wife He wants you to be—one who is capable of loving a less-than-perfect spouse. And don't forget to pray for faith—faith to believe that God's promises in Scripture apply to you—and your marriage.

Appendix #2

Note: The following article was first published in the May 2, 2003 issue of *Today's Christian Woman*. I have had twenty-some articles on marriage published, but this one has received the most comments and emails from readers—even years later. Those comments helped paved the way for the writing of this book. Some of what's in this piece you have already read in the book, but I believe seeing the truths repeated here will help.

Tough Love

5 Keys To Staying Married (When You Feel Like Calling It Quits)

Though my husband, Randy, and I recently celebrated our twenty-sixth wedding anniversary, our marriage hasn't been filled with the wedded bliss you might expect from such a committed couple. Through the years, our relationship has weathered the storms of Randy's struggle with pornography and a volatile temper, my severe PMS and incessant need for control, and our unforgiving spirits.

I've battled *I-can't-live-another-day-with-this-man* feelings.

And Randy has said that on the days I "acted crazy" (during my PMS), he's thought, *I can't live like this the rest of my life.* Since we've never allowed divorce to be an option, on my most desperate days, I've cried out to God, "I can't go on!"

But thanks to God's faithfulness and resurrection power, we *have* gone on. While we've both relied on our deep faith in God, we've also hung in there partly because I have a stubborn streak that God's transformed into tenacity. And Randy's stint as a Marine instilled him with an *I-will-not-give-up-on-this-mission* mindset—in this case, his mission being staying married to me for a lifetime.

As I hear others make excuses for withdrawing love from their spouse, I think of the motto Randy learned in the Marines: "No excuses—just results."

Even though we continue to struggle at times, Randy and I still love each other very much. Here are some of the lessons I've learned about loving my spouse even in the tough times.

Adopt God's Perspective on Sin

One problem in our marriage was my mixed-up view of sin. My sins—being critical or judgmental, for example—seemed small and harmless to me compared to Randy's swearing, temper, or spending all his time in front of the television rather than with the kids and me. However, God showed me the error of this thinking when I read Jesus' words in Matthew 7:5: "... first take the plank out of your own eye, and then you will see clearly to remove the speck from your brother's eye." Begrudgingly, I noticed it didn't say, "Remove the *plank* from your own eye, and then you will see clearly to remove the plank from your brother's eye."

When I let God expose my motives and attitudes in the light of his Word, my sins always appear like planks, while Randy's sins grow smaller in comparison. God wants me to deal with *my* sins, not Randy's.

While Randy was in the Marines, he perfected the bad habit of swearing. He still occasionally lets loose a string of profanities. I worried about its negative influence on our children, particularly when they would utter a curse word. I remember one day praying haughtily, "Lord, deliver him from this evil habit." But then the Holy Spirit spoke to me, *What about your sins of the mouth*? Suddenly they came to mind—criticizing, complaining, gossiping. I cringed when I realized our children had picked up these sinful habits too. The truth hit me: My use of words was no better than Randy's.

Now I see that Randy and I are equals as we each battle to overcome sinful habits in our lives. I feel so close to Randy when we help each other do this in an atmosphere of love, not condemnation.

Remember Who The Real Enemy of Marriage Is

In our second year of marriage, when Randy and I were further apart emotionally than we've ever been and I had nowhere else to go, I turned to God for salvation. In his mercy, God allowed the distance between Randy and me to open my heart to his saving grace.

As a believer, I continually need to remember that the enemy of my marriage isn't Randy, it's Satan. God's shown me the importance of being wise to the Enemy's schemes (2 Corinthians 2:11) and taking my stand against them (Ephesians 6:11). One way I do that is to remember what first caused me to fall in love with Randy—his faith in God, compassion, integrity, intelligence, wisdom, and great sense of humor. He still excels in these qualities, but too often I fail to focus on them.

One reason I kept seeing Randy as my enemy was that I

kept track of everything he did wrong. I even wrote down his "crimes"—his critical remarks, his lack of attentiveness toward me, for instance—on paper. Now when I start to make that list, God reminds me that love "keeps no record of wrongs" (1 Corinthians 13:5).

These days, I've decided to thank Randy for what he does *right*. I keep a record of these good things by daily jotting down something about Randy for which I'm thankful in my quiet-time journal. Sometimes I put these positives in a letter to Randy.

Occasionally when I slip back into *he's-the-enemy* thinking, Randy will say, "Honey, you're forgetting — we're a team." I appreciate his reminder, because I forget it all too often. We're partners working together to build a strong union and working against the enemy who aims to destroy marriages.

Pray God's Way

Instead of demanding that God do what I want in my husband's life, I've learned to ask, "How should I pray for Randy?" Then God gives me instructions and directs my prayers. One day I prayed, "How can I show love to Randy today?" I received a surprising answer: *Iron his shirts*. Randy knows I hate to iron, so that was a good way to show love. Even though it seemed to be such a little thing to me, Randy appeared so happy when he discovered me ironing his clothes.

Often during my prayer times, God uses his Word to bring me insights about true love. One verse he repeatedly brings to mind is 1 Corinthians 13:5, "It (love) is not self-seeking."

Love Your Husband Unconditionally

Recently I complained to God that he still hadn't answered a few specific prayers about Randy I've been praying for years.

I recalled two of Randy's habits that almost caused me to call off our wedding while we were engaged—his temper and his excessive television watching.

During that time, my attitude was, *I'll love you again if you change.* Randy wrote me letters promising he would. And he did—for a while.

Throughout the years of our marriage, I'm ashamed to admit I've sometimes waved those letters in front of him, demanding, "When are you going to keep your promises?" God convicted me that I still had a negative attitude and was holding back because of those habits. But *I'll love you fully if you change in those two areas* isn't in line with my marriage vows. The correct attitude is, *I love you even if these two things never change.*

Because of my wrong attitude, I've sometimes blocked the way for change, or been blind to how much Randy *has* changed—even in those two areas. And I've blocked the flow of love from my heart to Randy's.

One wise wife said, "My job's to love my husband; God's job is to change him." God wants me to love Randy fully and extravagantly, regardless of where he is in our life journey. After all, that's the way God loves us—unconditionally.

Give Your Marriage To God

Just because I pray for our marriage doesn't mean I always succeed in giving my difficulties to God. I'm quite adept at praying feverishly about problems and then taking them back one second after my "amen." My Bible study teacher has taught me to pray, "God, *you've* got a problem," which keeps me from thinking I have to solve everything.

The day I finally trusted God with my husband's addiction to pornography was a turning point in his healing. Prior to that point, I'd think Randy had given up viewing pornography only to find hidden contraband in our home.

"When is he ever going to give this up?" I'd cry to God, my counselor, or to a trusted friend. I told Randy my feelings, and he seemed to understand my hurt. I felt he finally was delivered.

But one morning I awoke early, and there was my husband looking at porn on the Internet. I felt as though I'd been kicked in the stomach. My usual response to such a discovery was sobbing, shouting, blaming, and shaming. This time I heard God whisper, *Say nothing.*

I went into the bathroom, knelt on the floor, and cried out, "God, I can't take this anymore."

Suddenly peace overwhelmed me as I gave Randy's sin and my pain to God. *Psalm 62:1* came to mind: "For God alone my soul waits in silence; from him comes my salvation" (AMP). For the first time, I was silent. I didn't say anything to Randy. I didn't complain to my friends. I didn't call my counselor. Instead, God helped me see Randy's battle rather than focus on how his addiction affected me. While Randy looked to pornography for comfort, I realized I too looked for comfort in things besides God—things such as food and shopping. Within a week, Randy announced, "I've made an appointment with a counselor," something I'd pleaded with him to do many times.

He confessed he'd never sought counseling before because he was ashamed. And what was my natural response when I caught him in the act? To shame him. *I* had been part of the problem.

When I got out of the way, Randy was able to turn to God for healing. Giving our marriage to God isn't a one-time deal; it's something I have to do over and over.

Recently my parents reached their fiftieth wedding anniversary. As I joined in celebrating their lasting love for each other, I reflected on God's faithfulness through their tough times. And ours. I'm looking forward to *our* fiftieth. We only have 24 more years to go. When Randy and I reach that milestone, I'll give God the credit. I'll shout, "What a miracle!"—and even more loudly, "What a Miracle Worker!"

EMMA CHAMBERS is a pen name for an author, inspirational speaker, former radio show host, and blogger who lives in the southeast. She has written for numerous Christian magazines such as *Decision, Today's Christian Woman, Light and Life* as well as for her town's daily and weekly newspapers. She writes of her personal experiences in articles and poems to show how God intervenes in her life. She also writes articles about spiritual growth and social issues. Because of her heart for the mentally ill and her own healing from clinical depression, for the past sixteen years, Emma has worked as a mental health tech on the psychiatric ward at a local hospital.

To contact Emma for questions, prayer requests, or encouragement, email her at emmachambers53@gmail.com